MW01031375

BARREN

&

Beloved

Dee Dee,

May blessings and love
fill your heart as
you read this story.
all my love

Cindy G. Steeves *Cindy*

Psalm 119:105

Trilogy Christian Publishers
A Wholly Owned Subsidiary of Trinity Broadcasting Network
2442 Michelle Drive
Tustin, CA 92780

Copyright © 2021 by Cindy G. Steeves
All Scripture quotations, unless otherwise noted, taken from
THE HOLY BIBLE, NEW INTERNATIONAL VERSION®,
NIV® Copyright © 1973, 1978, 1984, 2011 by Biblica, Inc.®
Used by permission. All rights reserved worldwide.
Scripture quotations marked (KJV) taken from The Holy Bible,
King James Version. Cambridge Edition: 1769.
All rights reserved, including the right to reproduce this book or
portions thereof in any form whatsoever.
For information, address Trilogy Christian Publishing
Rights Department, 2442 Michelle Drive, Tustin, Ca 92780.
Trilogy Christian Publishing/ TBN and colophon are trademarks
of Trinity Broadcasting Network.
For information about special discounts for bulk purchases,
please contact Trilogy Christian Publishing.
Manufactured in the United States of America

10 9 8 7 6 5 4 3 2 1
Library of Congress Cataloging-in-Publication Data is available.
ISBN 978-1-63769-130-4
ISBN 978-1-63769-131-1 (ebook)

DEDICATION

This is dedicated foremost to my Heavenly Father, who knew and understood me completely before I took one breath. My Lord, who paid the highest price for my freedom, who has won me completely. To McKenzie and Liberty, may you two beauties know the Father's love far sooner and far deeper than myself. To Lance and Lucas, two men in my life who only love one way, with hearts wide open.

ACKNOWLEDGMENTS

Mom and Dad, you prayed for me through the rough parts of my story and always left a light on for me to come home. Sharon, your friendship was the beginning of getting the words on paper. You never stopped believing in me. Melody, you are the sister of my heart. Faithful through the crying, rejoicing, and laughter. Mona, you are a precious gift from God. Your encouragement gave me the courage to publish. Are we not the sum of all the hearts we have loved? Thank you, many beautiful friends, for loving me back.

TABLE OF CONTENTS

PREFACE

The first time I heard the word *infertile*, I felt like the jury unanimously pronounced the verdict *unworthy*. Sure, I wanted to be fixed, healed. I desperately wanted the doctor to be wrong, but as I floundered through seasons of barrenness, what I needed was a friend, someone to say, "I know. It's not your fault." Loneliness was the heaviest secret I carried. My desire in telling my story is to be a friend to you.

Infertility will test your marriage. It can make you question your identity; it will bring you face to face with the question, "Who is God to me?" Are you praying for a baby miracle? I pray you will find your arms full and your heart whole. God is committed to loving you for life. Can anything conquer a woman who knows she is truly loved?

When I have the pleasure of getting to know new couples, I am guilty of requesting their story. Where did you meet? Was it love at first sight or denial? How did the proposal go? What is your secret to staying together? It feeds my soul to hear the unique ways we find each other. I wish we could sit together on comfy couches. I would have a steaming cup of coffee, and you, with your beverage of choice, would tell me your story. Often our life story has parallels to our God story. This is mine.

INTRODUCTION

Our ladies were gathered for a planning meeting. We were a small church in Edmonton, Alberta, in a lower-income community. The building showed its age. It was in desperate need of remodeling, from the paint-peeling signage to the chunky additions. The last renovation attempt lay incomplete from ten years prior. I found myself in this planning circle because Lance, my husband, had recently joined the church staff as the youth pastor. Sharon, our leader, Betty, Fiona, Nikki, and I were just as desperate for change. We began praying for the women of our church. Our prayers began stiff and formal but suddenly turned into a powerful prayer time. It was one of those times when you knew the Holy Spirit was present. You didn't just feel unity of purpose, unity was there.

Sharon was praying about our upcoming ladies' retreat. Maybe if we could convince all of our ladies to attend, God would birth change. She prayed, "Lord, let all ages of ladies come; let all ages and stages of life be welcome."

I wholly agreed, "Yes, Lord."

Sharon went on to pray, "Lord, you are the God of Abraham, Isaac, and Jacob."

At that very moment, the Holy Spirit whispered to me, "Cindy, I am also the God of Sarah, Rebecca, and Rachel!"

My spirit leaped. I just knew he was letting me know my season of barrenness was coming to an end. I would finally conceive a baby!

1.

∾

HOME

"Those who look to him are radiant; their faces are never covered with shame"

(Psalm 34:5)

❝Take a deep breath and cough for me." The cold stethoscope suited his tone of voice. I squeaked out a cough so weak that Dr. Greening laughed indignantly and said, "Come on. You've got to do better than that." Feeling completely mocked, I decided right then and there that I hated him; I hated his utter lack of sympathy for why I was there and for his ability to make me feel like a child. I was angry that I needed a person like this in my life, that he was supposed to be one of the best at this horrible process. I thought of the walls covered in photos of babies. The hallways were lined with them; you couldn't miss the fact that many photos had twins and some triplets. So what if he just saw me and my husband as another payday for his selfish life. I could put up with his tasteless jokes about being an alcoholic because he had something I wanted as well. This may be my last chance.

"It's too bad you waited so long to come here. The chances of conceiving are low at your age." (Translation: "You're old!") "This will be quite a costly procedure because people like yourself won't lobby the government for funding." (Translation: "I hope you're set up to pay big bucks!") I felt a tad smug at this point. We weren't shocked; we had done our research. Canada has free basic healthcare, but *in vitro* would be a fully out-of-pocket expense. Finally, the ultimate, matter-of-fact disclaimer: "There are no guarantees." (Translation: "We win every time, but you, my dear, your chances are not favorable.")

As I was considering an indignant reply to this horrid man, I was interrupted ever so gently by the voice I had grown to love. My Lord, with his perfect timing, whispered, "You know you won't go through with this if your head is in this space. You've come too far, beloved, to default to those old ways. Will you stop viewing people as enemies? I know you are afraid, but I am here, and no matter what happens, that will not change."

Slowly exhaling, I looked past his robotic shell that made me feel like I was on a conveyor belt and into Dr. Greening's eyes. I could see he was just holding it together; I could see his pain. All my judgments evaporated. "Dr. Greening, I just want to thank you for your time. I bet it's hard doing this job and seeing so many desperate couples every day."

He softened for a split second but quickly recouped with more sarcasm. "The thing is, we can do what we can, but only God can make a baby!" If he thought to ground me with that reality, he did not succeed. To think that no human could take the credit only lightened my heart. The peace of feeling God's presence was something I was not willing to trade for anyone or anything ever again. It was the only thing from my childhood of value, and now that I had it back, I continually guarded it.

As we left the appointment, I noticed a big, hard-cover *Cinderella* storybook amongst the magazines in the waiting room. It seemed out of place because there would be no need for distractions for children in this place, would there? In the car, we buckled up and settled in for the three-hour drive home. I put in earbuds to listen to music and enjoy a nap, but thoughts of that book interrupted me. What was it about that book? Ah, that's it! A memory was triggered. Now I remembered that when I was in third grade, a boy in my class gave it to me in a Christmas gift exchange. Wow, I loved that book; I bet I read it a thousand times. I began to think about the story, and I felt the Lord say, "Let's remember together." I smiled at recognizing the pattern of how he uses the smallest glimpse to get my attention. At the moment, it seemed small, but in hindsight, that glimpse was a megaphone. So, I remembered with him as he showed me his relentless heart at every turn.

I sang the song over and over every single day. The skipping rope swiped the ground in a methodic rhythm. "Cinderella, Cinderella, went upstairs to kiss a fella. Made a mistake and kissed a snake. How many doctors did it take?"

To a child, what you experience in childhood is normal. Well, it's your normal; you haven't seen enough to know you are different. I could feel God in the warm rays of the sunshine, I could smell his nearness in the salty air, and I could hear his voice inside me. Back then, living in the eastern Atlantic cove, I didn't try to figure it out or understand why or how. It was just beautifully normal.

Arnold's Cove, Newfoundland, was a small fishing settlement on the Avalon Peninsula. For an eight-year-old, it was paradise. My next-door neighbor and best friend was Tanya, and she had introduced herself by saying, "Want to come see my puppies?" Her house was raised, so we walked into the enclosed ground level, similar to a basement. I was astonished to see a wooden crate with a golden dog and eight whimpering puppies, which I could smell before my eyes adjusted to the dim light. (My mom did not like animals; you would never find this at my house.) If that weren't enough to make me giddy for weeks, Tanya held out her hands to show me what she was holding: a kitten! Her cat also had a litter at the same time as her dog. I thought Tanya was the richest girl in the world. Best of friends, we would search the beach for treasures of ocean smoothed glass, shells, and marbled rocks. We would spend hours swinging at the park and running through the tall grass.

If my grandmother asked me to go to the store for her, there was always a quarter for me to spend, and it was enough to buy a generous amount of candy to sustain the day's adventures. With the pink rubber skipping rope looped over one shoulder, my heels scuffed on the loose gravel. While walking up the road back home, I could see my yellow house. You couldn't tell if anyone was home from the outside, but I knew not to be late for dinner.

My conversation with God began: "God, can I tell you something? It's something that I wish, but I know it's wrong to wish for."

"You can tell me anything and everything, and especially the wrong things. What is it, my sweet child?"

"I don't want to grow up. I love jumping rope and walking on the beach. Oh, and swings. I love swings. And it seems to me that grownups are not very happy. I wish you made it so we didn't have to grow up."

"Oh, Cindy, the reason you are not excited to grow up is because you can't see what I see. You are nervous because you have never been there. You don't know all the gifts I have waiting for you. You will be a lady who is full of joy, and you will never stop skipping."

I responded with a burst of laughter at the thought of my mom skipping. "Thank you, God. I guess I was scared because I didn't remember that you would be with me. I would never want to live without you in my life."

Peaceful words settled my heart as I heard his whisper, "I will never leave you or forsake you."

As I ran up the high wooden steps to the front door, the smell of fresh bread made my mouth water before I could even kick off my sneakers.

"Sit down. Supper is ready," Mom said in her calm way.

When everyone was seated, we were told the terrible news that a cousin much older than I had died. He had driven a car off a government wharf. A terrible accident! The adults were shocked and quiet. It was the first time I heard the word *drowned*. I did not know this cousin very well, I didn't go to the funeral, and I did not cry one tear. I had only one response. I walked outside and down the gravel road until I could see the government wharf; it looked like a fortress compared to the man-made fishing stages that backed off the private homes scattering the coastline. It was wide enough to drive on and had the feel of a town square.

I began to speak. "God, did you hear what happened?"

"Yes, I did." There was no hesitation in his tone.

"When I grow up, I pretty much have to drive a car, and that makes me so scared. I know what I will do if I have a boyfriend, and he wants to drive me somewhere. I will make him drive from here way down to that big wharf and back before he can drive me anywhere."

"Cindy, you are awfully young to build walls of protection for yourself. You need only to trust me. Don't be afraid. The man I have for you will be a place of safety in and out of cars. He will go much further than the short distance you have pointed out to conquer your heart, and he will be an excellent driver."

"You always do that, God. You more than answer my questions; you answer my heart."

From that day on, I knew I would fall in love. I dreamed of being a bride; I dreamed of weddings and, of course, Prince Charming. That day it was as if God gave me a puzzle piece that would fit only one other piece. How I wish now I could say that man with the connecting piece was the only one I gave my heart to.

In 1976, the oil refinery where my dad worked went into receivership and closed. Unemployment soared, and the local economy suffered a death blow. My dad tried his hand at reupholstering furniture, then repairing sewing machines. I went along with him on one of his calls to repair a machine and the elderly lady mistook me for a boy because of my short haircut. Commented to my dad about what a nice son he had. Adding insult to injury, my father replied, "Thank you!" In his defense, I do have two brothers, but they were not with us. I decided right there my mother would no longer cut my hair; I would be better off doing it myself. My mom worked as a waitress. It wasn't easy to think of these as hard times when one of the benefits of her job was milkshakes for us when we had to pick her up.

All my parents' efforts to make a new living were futile. "The economy is not coming back anytime soon," my dad explained. I didn't understand what that meant. I just knew we were moving far away—over three thousand miles. There was no Internet back then to learn about the northern oil town we were moving to. There was just packing, flying, and the lost feeling that I had left something very important behind.

When I said the name, "Fort McMurray," it felt like I was mumbling. It was a strange place. Instead of the ocean, there was a dense forest right across from our home, and one day we saw a black bear with two little cubs just toddling along. A valuable sighting, it gave me a healthy fear of wandering into the forest.

This community was growing faster than I could spin coins at a candy machine. My third-grade class was increasing by one or two new students every week for a few months. Miss King, my teacher, was constantly correcting my Newfie (Newfoundland) accent. "It's not 'ear'; it's 'here,'" she would say. Newfies drop H's from some words and add them to others. I could have accepted her critiques if it weren't for the fact she was from Australia and often had twenty-five sets of eyes looking at her in bewilderment because of her accent. That was the interesting thing about Fort McMurray: it seemed no one was actually from there. Mostly, my brothers and I were content because there was a Kentucky Fried Chicken in this new community. What says status more than that?

2.

∽

HOMELESS

*"Do not gloat over me, my enemy! Though I have fallen,
I will rise. Though I sit in darkness, the Lord will be my
light"*

(Micah 7:8)

I am so grateful for the memories of early childhood;
they are a gift I cherish. Sadly, the easiness of per-
ceiving God's heart for me diminished in strength, and
I know why.

He was a charismatic and respected friend of our
family who laughed a lot. In fact, in a room full of
socializing adults, he would be the last person you
would expect to violate a child. The first time it happened, I was nine. In my head, I was screaming, but
no sound came from my mouth. Like in a nightmare,
I was running with all my might, but my feet were
stuck in quicksand. My brain completely disconnect-

ed from what was happening; I had nothing to draw on to understand. I instinctively knew it was terribly wrong, and if I had reacted by telling my parents, it would have ended. Unfortunately, I thought that if I did tell, this man, whom everyone loved, would be ruined because of the trouble I caused. Something in me took responsibility; shame entered and became a part of me. One of the many lies I believed was that it was a mistake, and it would never happen again.

A reasonable reaction would be to become a person of fear who distanced from men, but I was not reasonable. Throughout high school, I discovered that I felt powerful and in control by being the one who chose to throw my heart away over and over. I believed there was nothing special about me worth saving. You only get one heart, and by the time high school was over, mine was battered. The strong presence of God had become a faint mist. The ache in my heart was so painfully constant.

I heard a new voice now; it wasn't like the gentle whisper I used to hear when I was young. It was a low, nervous, hum-like vibration: "You're not thinking of talking to him, are you? You know where you are is all your fault, right? Of course, he's God. He will take you back, but you've got to at least try to clean yourself up a little. You even look pathetic. Show him you're serious and willing to work at it. And what a lot of work to do; my, you've made a mess."

I agreed it was undeniably my fault. I was a mess and oh so far away. The thought of cleaning myself up was exhausting. I hadn't heard God's voice in so long. At that time, I believed God couldn't be around sin, and I wore it like a red jumpsuit. God was holy. How could a holy God come close to me? I understood that, but it hurt.

The best way to protect from being hurt ever again is to become cold. At first, it takes practice, but eventually, you become numb, and then it's easy. There is a high cost to this protection: you can keep all pain from touching you, but no warmth can enter such a barren place. You can see; you can hear; you just can't feel. I pushed away everyone who loved me and moved out of my parents' home. I had a place to stay—an apartment, sofa, bed, and a table—but I felt homeless. I found if I could keep busy, I wouldn't feel empty. So, I was as busy as a nineteen-year-old could be. Every day was the same: gray and static. While alone one afternoon, I felt something change. He was there, right there, as large as life. I was caught off guard, but I knew it was God.

I heard him so clearly: "Cindy, my heart is still for you. Won't you talk to me?"

"How can I even be hearing you? You are righteous, but I am defiled by my own choices. Is it really you, God?"

"I am everywhere; there is no place you can go where I am not, even to the furthest ocean. Don't you remember? I will never leave you or forsake you."

"I thought it was more like you could see everything that happens as in the song lyric, 'Be careful little hands what you do.'"

"Cindy, it means so much more. I will never forsake, never relinquish, never let go."

I don't know how I could have resisted his appeal except that the consistent practice of coldness had become my armor, so I didn't feel. I just responded. "God, I'm asking you to please stop talking to me. I've decided not to be close to you. I don't trust anyone in my life, and I don't want to hear you. You only confuse me." The coldness became normal, and the normal became quiet. I did not hear him speak; God obliged my request.

In the next two years, I became an expert at not being good. I made every decision based on whatever way the wind was blowing. I didn't care about what was best for me or anyone. Every step was a stumble. I was empty.

If you ask Jesus to stop talking, he may agree as he did with me, but one thing you can be sure of: he will never leave you. He cannot leave any more than you can will your heart to stop beating. I could feel him watching me in agony. Many times, he wanted to rescue me, but I would not bid him come.

One night, I had fallen into a dark stupor. I was literally lying on the mucky ground, numb and intoxicated. My guard was low, my shame was high, and the words moaned out of my mouth, "Why don't you leave me and let me die? I don't care; why should you?"

He spoke no words; he just constantly watched over me, over my haunted brokenness. Why could I not disgust him when I had become so disgusted with myself?

I awoke to the reality that I had lost everything, although I didn't have much to start with. I had lost my job; I had no money, no friends, and no purpose. I had sold all my possessions, including a ring from my parents; a daughter's pride ring that had our three birthstones. In truth, I felt like I sold my soul. I bought a little more time of being in control of my vacant world. Nothing changed.

Now I wanted to go home, but that loud and clear mocking voice said, "The only way you could sink lower than you are right now would be to believe you deserve a second chance! God tried to warn you, but now things are so much worse than before, aren't they?"

Yes, things were worse. I felt every step of those three thousand miles from my childhood home.

God weaves in and through our circumstances in mysterious ways. The person who was the biggest offender of my heart was the one God used to deliver an invitation to come back to my Lord. I had deeply buried the past abuse from my childhood. Because I had never told anyone, it was like it never happened. I believed that the immoral choices I made were worse than anything that had been done to me. My present pain was paramount. An old friend invited me out for dinner, and I was so hungry that it did not phase me that the man who had violated me would be there; those incidents were not even on my radar. The truth is that I was more desperate than repentant, but God knew that when he extended the invitation. My dear friend wasted no time in pointing out the obvious: my life was a wreck.

I responded with the weakest defense: "I have done so much that I can't see how God would accept my prayers." The smell of cigarette smoke on my clothing wafted to my own nostrils and sickened me; this was confirmation!

The man at the table spoke, "Cindy, we all have deep regrets. God can forgive anything!" Our eyes met, and in that instant, faint memories surfaced. I had a rush of thoughts, *Was he talking about himself? Was he somehow apologizing? Was he right; did we all have horrid darkness in us?* I had a flash of Jesus looking at the thief on the cross and then looking at his weeping mother. I understood; Jesus loved them both. Completely. Hope, like a smoldering wick, exposed the smallest crack in my protective walls, and I wondered if it were true. Could I change? Desperate people can't afford pride, so I just went for it. I breathed out a frail prayer; I still felt unsure but with peace bubbles.

The very next thing I did was tell my parents—at two a.m. on their doorstep. I reassured myself by thinking if my repentance didn't stick, I had nothing to lose. I also pronounced this disclaimer to my parents, who were rejoicing like the house was paid for; it's hard to convince parents who had been persistent in prayer to not get too excited.

Before I spoke one repentant word, a blanket of grace wrapped around me, and I knew it was real. "God, why are you so kind to me?"

"Cindy, you have the rest of your life to understand that, and you will because I am going to show you the depth of my faithfulness."

"Even if you never spoke another word to me, Lord, you have shown me more faithfulness than I deserve."

"I no longer call you servant. I call you daughter. You don't get a wage or a portion; all that I have is yours."

That night, I had the best sleep of my life. I dreamed I was the Prodigal Son. I was far away from home, so far from who I was, that my very appearance was distorted. I was in a completely different country. While I was yet so far away, he was waiting and watching for me every day. I did not know this. I decided to go back, not because I was repentant, but because I was desperate, desperate for food, desperate to survive. It would be a long journey, but the journey to nowhere would be further.

I could see in the distance the boundary of my family's land, and it looked like paradise. I continued to put one foot in front of the other solely on the truth that my father was just. He was known for fairness toward all. If I could convince him to take me back as a servant, I would never feel hunger again. I saw someone running toward me. A scout? My brother? Was my brother coming to gloat? As he neared, I recognized the posture of the approaching man. Was that my father? Has he come to personally drive me away?

I was wasted and ashamed, but in truth, my heart was still hard. I was ready to negotiate. I had rehearsed my lines over and over along the way, but before I could utter one word, he pulled me to his chest. I will never forget his cry, the sound of his anguished heart reviving. I could hear his booming heartbeat; he smelled of spices and fresh bread. His embrace was a flood to my dry, stony heart, and I began to weep and weep. With each expanse of his lungs, my heart collapsed. He held my jaw until I looked right into his eyes. My father smothered my face, full of days of dust and salty tears, with his kisses.

My voice cracked with the stammering of my unfaithfulness. The speech I had rehearsed over and over on the way back, I could not recall. "Mercy on me; mercy on me," were the only words I could manage. My father's garment became soaked and soiled because of my filth. I became aware of the stench of my clothing against his clean robes. I tried to put space between us by kneeling before him, but he would not release me. He called to his servants to bring a robe for me. While one ran for the robe, he sent another to bring shoes and a ring! He pulled my shredded rags away, and I was swiftly covered in dignity in his robe. I was home.

I woke up to find that his grace was real, my heart was clean, and clean felt free. I didn't know one thing about my future, but I knew I was loved. The reality was no longer to be escaped but a treasure to be chased.

One benefit that I had from high school was three years of Beauty Culture electives. As God would have it, a door opened for me to get the apprenticeship hours I needed to get a hairstylist license. I was never deeply passionate about the latest fashion and cutting-edge hairstyles, but I did enjoy visiting with people, and that was half the job description. I landed in a tiny, four-chair salon in the small town my parents were pastoring in. My Lord's voice returned to me, and his presence was always near. The Holy Spirit alerted my attention to those around me who needed a kind word or represented a lesson I could learn. He seemed to be continually affirming his love for me.

I was washing a client's hair, one of my main tasks as an apprentice. (As an apprentice, I rinsed so many perms that the smell of ammonia became soothing.) Most clients would lie back and just enjoy the lathering scalp massage, but this lady was not relaxed. She was clearly puzzling over something that bothered her. She had a ton of thick, mousy brown hair that took longer to wash, and then it needed rewashing and conditioning. I knew to comb the conditioner through, or there would be a mess of tangles and then more rinsing. As I worked, I prayed silently that God would show his love for her, that he would calm her, and show her she was beautiful to him.

As I raised the chair back and supported her monumental towel-wrapped head, a man rose from the seating area to join her. He squatted down to her level beside the chair and said, "Hi, Baby." His long red hair suited his hippie tone. She nearly collapsed on his shoulder, comforted by the nearness of his face. "What's the matter, baby?" He wasn't surprised by her excessive reaction; he was so calming. She melted, and that's when all her puzzling spilled out. I was a captive audience to the conversation because he was kneeling by the shampoo chair, and I was blocked in. They were not put off by my presence. Through her hand-covered face, she poured out how she had just come from a Weight Watchers meeting, and she was up three pounds. (I wanted to suggest that a serious haircut would fix that problem but knew the timing was not right.) She then went on to inform this tender-hearted man that she now weighed ten pounds heavier than Arnold Schwarzenegger!

He placed his rough hand on her cheek and replied, "And you are absolutely beautiful to me!"

I'm sure God allowed me to witness this to remind me what love sounds like and awaken the desire in my heart again.

It was a sweet season of being at home again. I achieved my apprentice hours, passed the exams, and earned a stylist license. I found a job in the city at a department store salon and two roommates to share the rent. I was ready for independence the right way.

3.

⌒

HOUSE OF HOPE

*"You make known to me the path of life; you will fill me
with joy in your presence, with eternal pleasures at your
right hand"*

(Psalm 16:11)

It is amazing that what seems to be the most medi-
ocre of days can become the day your life changes
forever.

I went to work in the same way, did three perms,
two cuts, five shampoo-sets, and went home in the exact same way, fully expecting to do the same the next
day. After I pounded up the deteriorating concrete
steps to our walk-up apartment, I found that one of my
roommates had invited friends over. Full disclosure:
they had been on a double date. She was paired with
a guy to keep the other couple company. After recov-
ering from literally tripping over my own two feet, it

37

happened: I was introduced to the one who was the perfect fit for my puzzle piece, and I had no idea it was him. Well, truthfully, I found him to be handsome: distractingly handsome, too handsome for me. He was tall, over six feet, with dark wavy hair, and he wore a leather letterman jacket that was dark denim in color, the kind of jacket a guy lends a girl who's cold, and it swims around her. Lance. I had never met anyone named Lance before; I liked it. He was attractive because he was fearless—not a self-conscious bone in his body! He intrigued me because he wasn't egotistical either. He was an absolutely wonderful mystery. I felt eight again, surrounded by puppies and kittens! He told funny stories that had the room captured with delight. For a crazy St. Bernard imitation, he took a large gulp of water and, without swallowing, yelled, "Woof," the water spraying everyone who leaned in to hear the punch line. We all roared. There was a subtle clue that should have alerted me. When he spoke to me, he looked right into my eyes, and I could see. I could see he was honest.

That night, I went to bed and journaled as always. I felt myself smiling on the inside as I wrote, "Lord, just so you know, he is exactly what I am looking for!"

Of course, I wrote it totally tongue-in-cheek because I thought him too wonderful for me. I was so grateful for God's grace, but I believed any future relationship for me would not be with someone so good. Lance deserved a girl who, like him, didn't have a messy history. God couldn't change my past. I believed I had to live with my consequences, and I was okay with that.

I was pleasantly surprised to see Lance over the next few weeks at different events, but I was still completely oblivious to the potential of a relationship. He even came to my salon for a haircut; I dropped my scissors, twice! Way too many obstacles stood between us: I was three years older, he was out west just for school and lived two thousand miles away, I was just finding my way with God, and he was going to be a pastor! Yes, we were worlds apart.

Walks and talks turned into dates. For our first official date, he called me and asked if I wanted to go out for dinner, just the two of us. I'm sure he could hear my heart beating over the phone, trying desperately to sound casual as I said, "Sure! Sounds great." Then he proceeded to explain it would happen in two weeks after he got paid! It meant the world to me that he cared enough to secure the date. It was a humble and charming beginning. Dates turned into meeting each other's families. I was still protecting my heart, so I would tell everyone it was casual. This earned Lance the nickname "Casual Lance," but honestly, I was ruined for anyone else. I felt completely comfortable, safe, and electric with anticipation. Time spent together was never long enough. We were out for a walk one night (because walks didn't cost a thing), and we stopped and sat at a spot overlooking the river valley. I'm sure the stars were out, and the view was grand, but I could only look at him. Could one person really be God's perfect plan? The feeling of not being able to save myself swam over me. "My, he's great," I thought to myself, half praying it.

Lance said, "Cindy, I wish I could ask you to marry me tonight, but the truth is, I can't even buy a ring, not to mention paying for a wedding."

To know you are loved and desired is a greater value than any possession you can hold in your hands. He was so vulnerable, and I completely melted. We prayed and told God how we felt and trusted his timing to be perfect.

I didn't know until months later, but that very night, Lance got a call from his dad saying, "Son, it's not my way to pry, but I just want you to know that I have this ring from your grandfather and if you would like to have the diamond reset for an engagement ring for Cindy, it's yours." How many gifts are our heavenly Daddy just waiting for us to ask him for? He wants to lavish us with kindness beyond our expectations.

Lance was in his second year of seminary; his plan was to stay out west to work that summer instead of going back to his home in Ontario. He told me his parents offered to pay for our airfare to visit for a couple of weeks, and we could help cover the expense by working with his dad. It sounded like a great deal, and I wanted to keep my side of it. Every morning I was greeted with a new plan of touring around to take in the sights. I kept asking when I was going to work to help with the airfare, but the inquiry was always brushed off. Strange. One morning I heard the plan for the day was to visit Niagara Falls. I was so excited; I had been there once before at Christmas, in the evening. The park was decorated in lights, and the falls were lit up. It was spectacular then, but now I'd get to see it in the sunshine. I heard there is a guaranteed rainbow over horseshoe falls when the sun is shining.

We stopped for lunch on the way to a restaurant

called Plain and Fancy. Everything was perfection. I was reeling with happiness. Lance gave me a single red rose. It did not even occur to me to consider where he got this rose. The server asked if we would like anything else, like coffee, at the end of our meal. I was just about to say yes, please, and he cut in with, "No thanks. We've got to get going." I don't know if I was the dedicated coffee lover than I am today or if I was just miffed that he didn't even ask what I wanted to do. Not one of my finer moments: I pouted the rest of the drive like a four-year-old denied ice cream. He tried to coax me out of this foul mood by repeating a question he asked me almost daily, "If I were to ask you to marry me today, what would you say?"

I would usually respond with something like, "Oh, honey! Yes, yes, double yes." But today's response was, "Well, I don't know what I would say. We will have to wait until that day gets here and find out then!" This shows how completely unsuspecting I was of the order of events Lance had planned.

Thirty minutes later, we arrived at the three magnificent falls that make up Niagara: American Falls, Bridal Veil Falls, and Horseshoe Falls, where we settled to enjoy the view. The 176-foot falls on the Canadian side has thirty-one thousand tons of water surging over the rim every second at a speed of forty-two miles per hour. I was captivated. I had never been so close to that magnitude of power and beauty. The contrast of the hot sun and cold mist felt holy. I thought, "How could anyone stand here and not believe in God?" I was in awe of my Creator. I relaxed and drank in the wonder that surrounded me.

Lance's sister, Nadine, was also there. She ran into the little souvenir shop to get a drink. She was fifteen years old, so it did not strike me as one bit strange that she returned with fortune cookies! (Teenagers are random that way.) They coaxed me, still clueless, into reading my fortune first for the rolling video camera. The beauty that surrounded me softened my mood, but I was still a little chilly toward Lance; I would not comply. "Lance, read yours first," I said in a bossy tone.

He cracked the cookie open and, with a robotic voice, said, "Cindy will be mine. Oh yes, she will be mine." He then stuffed the cookie and the fortune into his mouth and ate the whole thing. He was always doing those kinds of antics.

So, I'm next. I snapped my cookie open, pulled out the tiny paper, and read the type-written words to myself: "Will you marry me?"

A normal, healthy response would be to read it out loud, scream, cry, hug, kiss, and celebrate. But my default response kicked in, and all my protective barriers went up to full force. Every sound stopped. I couldn't hear the roaring falls, or Lance's sister repeating over and over, "Read it!" My life was happy, even joyful, but there were still some deep wounds inside that had never healed, so the only way I could make sense of this was to conclude it was a joke, a very cruel joke. There was no way possible that he could actually propose. I looked up and saw the camera still rolling. I did not want to be humiliated.

"Cindy, read it out loud. What does it say?" he coaxed.

I would not be made fun of even if they didn't intend to be hurtful. All I could whisper was, "Is it true?"

Lance said, "I don't know. What does it say?" He planned to capture the moment forever on video. He was as full of joy as I was full of fear.

I looked into his eyes and pleaded, "Please just tell me. Is it true; is this real?"

At that moment, he dropped to his knees, pulled

out a brown velvet ring box, extended it toward me, and asked, "Will you be my wife?"

The dam broke. I felt as if the force of the falls exploded in my chest. It was real. He loved me and wanted me for the rest of my life. As I slumped into his arms, all protective barriers crumbled into a million tiny pieces. I was laughing at this impossible thing and then noticed that all the tourists who had also captured our moment were clapping and congratulating us.

On the drive back, I could feel the Lord's presence celebrating. "Cindy, I'm pleased to see this day with you and to see you truly overcome and open your heart to receive love."

We arrived back at Lance's parent's house for a family celebration, and the announcement of an engagement party set for the next day! Celebration was everywhere. The next morning, I woke up to find hot coffee and the newspaper waiting for me at the kitchen table.

Lance's mom, Rossanne, said, "Cindy, that is the Bolton Enterprise. It's a fabulous newspaper with the most exciting and up-to-date news! Her pride in the local paper seemed a little over the top, but maybe I just needed to drink the coffee first to process her patriotism. Nothing seemed extraordinary to me, then I turned to the next page. There was a photo of Lance and me. Thankful that I had already swallowed my last sip, and completely taken by surprise, I read of our engagement that happened just fourteen hours earlier and the congratulations of Lance's family. No wonder Lance was so committed to his plan; there was a lot riding on my yes. This made me think of how God planned the way to my heart, building steps that he himself would walk for me, so I could feel safe enough to trust him fully and receive his love forever.

Organization and planning are a passion of mine; one of my core values is order. This has shown up many times as control, but in balance, it grounds me and makes me happy. I have kept a journal since my teens, so the next important task would be to buy a special, fresh book that would hold all the designs and intentions for the perfect day to come. Weddings should be fun to plan. They are the celebration of new beginnings and the ceremony of promise.

Our minister for the ceremony was a dear friend of my parents and a prison chaplain. He met with us to give us a little advice, to see if we had questions, and to plan the particulars of our ceremony. We even had the experience of going to his office in a medium-security correctional center. The many checkpoints and locked gates we had to get through was a suitable foreshadow of the work required in a strong marriage. Pastor Garry was an expert at reading people. He told us about how inmates will appear to be sincere to win your trust and then try to get you to do something against the rules, like using a private phone line. If they succeed, they then have something to hold over you. Hearing his words in that very location served as a powerful warning to keep our hearts clean and guard our marriage.

I wonder what Pastor Garry was "reading" in me as our conversation transitioned to the question of our choice of vows? Lance automatically replied, "Traditional."

To which I put on the breaks by asking, "Do we really need the word obey? Is that really what our marriage is about?"

I would almost bet at that point Pastor Garry's intuition was shouting, "Lance, run away! Run away!" I was firm on the belief that marriage was fifty-fifty, and it was a partnership. Garry explained, "Cindy, there will be times in your marriage when you do not agree, and you will have to choose who leads. I'm not trying to get you to select traditional vows. I want you to see the bigger picture. Why is your heart resistant? Do you trust Lance?"

Lance was quiet; I was stubborn. I reaffirmed how my heart was 100 percent in. I loved Lance; I just needed to wait on the vow decision.

The next morning, I was in prayer, and as honestly as I could, I asked God, "Are you telling me I have to obey?"

In his way of drawing me into vulnerability, I felt him ask me, "Where do you think I will be at your wedding?"

This is confirmation of God's voice; he would ask something I could never imagine on my own. I thought about walking down the aisle. Would he be next to my father, giving me away? Nope, not there. Would he be standing by Pastor Garry as a witness? Nope. I imagined the guests, the pianist, the table where we would sign the marriage certificate, and then I gasped at the place my thoughts landed: the communion table! I imagined Jesus holding the cup and the bread. I had no words; in that imagined picture, I understood his heart. Marriage is a covenant, like communion is receiving his new covenant. My resistant heart just changed. I knew marriage wasn't a fifty-fifty partnership; it was 100 percent for both of us until death us do part. My trust needed to be in God's ability to lead Lance. I called Pastor Garry to choose traditional vows.

The wedding day was as it should be: perfect and full of bumps that became hilarious memories. July 23, 1994, was the hottest day of the year; my four bridesmaids did not share my joy in the choice of red velvet dresses! In our photos, they look like melting ice cream cones. The flower shop accidentally made a basket arrangement instead of loose rose petals for the flower girl. She was supposed to scatter the petals down the aisle, and no one noticed as the flower girl, committed to her job, pulled the arrangement apart bit by bit until the remains of green floral foam looked like a failed science project.

Lance thanked a friend for videotaping the ceremony. His reply was, "I didn't do anything, man!"

Thinking he was being modest, Lance responded, "Well, it may not be much to you, but it means a lot to us." We later found out he literally did nothing! We pieced together some shots from different family members, and we have a "memorable" video. The day was surrounded by friends and family, full of laughter and smiling until our cheeks cramped.

Like our wedding day, how often do our careful planning and attention to detail fade like a puff of smoke while the area of greatest importance, the actual marriage that endures long after the party, is ignored. We tend to focus on what we can see while the real value is in the things you can't buy or display. "So we fix our eyes not on what is seen, but on what is unseen, since what is seen is temporary, but what is unseen is eternal" (2 Corinthians 4:18). How I wish I had learned this back in the early days.

We found our first home. It was a one-bedroom apartment that we affectionately called "the love nest." The tiny galley kitchen had swinging saloon-like doors, and the living room had a real wood-burning fireplace. Our style of decor consisted of door-sized posters, and the bathroom door featured our finest piece: a black and white image of a young boy and girl dressed in whimsical clothes holding a red rose. It was cutting edge modern. Like pigs in mud, we thought we were in paradise. What more could two people want?

When you fall in love, and I mean the real deal, the kind that says, "Love is blind, but the neighbors ain't," this crazy thing happens. Giddiness takes prime real estate in your brain, and inhibitions and insecurity get pushed down. A free, uninhibited version of you rises to the occasion, and you are spontaneously led moment by moment. I know I am not the only one this has happened to because I have sat with other struggling young couples, and I hear from both sides, "This is not the same person I married; she used to be fun, exciting, happy..." In the state of new love, you feel fearless, your trust level is high, and you believe you are whole. I was not. Loving and opening my heart was proof that I wanted to be whole, not proof that I was.

So, here's where the saying, "The honeymoon is over," comes in. The way I was all tangled up inside had to resurface. It was just a matter of time. Soon, the wedding album lost its freshness, and everyday living settled in place of the constant enamoring. No man can succeed in making his wife feel like a bride every waking moment of every day, no matter how much that bride whines, acts out, and drains the life out of him. (Poor Lance.) And he is not supposed to.

There is and always will be only one who can be your source of life, and he is not your husband; he is God. How unfair to put Creator's expectations on a man. I like how Proverbs 21:9 in the Passion Translation states this verse: "It's better to live all alone in a rickety shack than to share a castle with a crabby spouse!" In our lives, it meant there was no house big enough to get away from the constant draining of an unhappy wife, and we were in a one-bedroom apartment!

The stage was perfectly set for the lying voice to return, and that it did. "I told you so." This next phrase seems so small, but it cut deep: "Who do you think you are?" It was subtle, but oh so familiar. The more I analyzed our marriage, the more I pondered what was missing, and the subtle phrase became powerful. It was a cloud of accusation that moved in front of the sun, the temperature dropped, it became a little darker, and I felt like I wanted to hide.

We had talked about everything before we got married, so we both knew we wanted children. Actually, we did not just want or would have liked children. We mutually agreed we were put on this earth to have children! Maybe that's it. If we had a baby, that would ignite that soulmate flame again. We had only been married a couple of months, but I decided to talk to Lance about my brilliant idea.

He did not hesitate; he just said, "Let's pray about

it." This is a great characteristic of my husband. He is very calm and focused, but that's like a balloon popper when you want someone to jump up and down and be crazy in the moment! Sure, I thought, what's to pray about? It's God's idea to multiply upon the earth, so we already know he wants us to do our part, and I just happen to be a math whiz, so bring on the multiplication! So, he prayed a simple prayer, or so I thought, "Lord, we would like to have a baby, and we trust your timing."

I was so excited. I felt like it was a done deal. We would be complete when we were a family, and I was quite sure it took at least three to make a family. All my ponderings were correct: the honeymoon was back on, we started laughing again, we had long talks about how many children we would have, how many boys, how many girls, which names we liked, which names were out because of potential teasing when they went to school, what kind of parents we would be, how our children would not be annoying like some people's kids, and what if we had twins! It was like planning how to spend the money from a lottery you had not won yet. I was attracted to every baby I saw; I would ask to hold new babies and comment on their darling features, all the while my uterus was screaming, "Fill me up." I'm sure I had a permanent grin as if I were carrying a grand secret that everyone was dying to know. I bought a pregnancy test because I was pretty sure the wonder was already happening inside of me. Yes, the silly love feeling was back, and soon our love nest would have a little hatchling, and it would prove I was someone.

4.

HOUSE OF
HOPELESSNESS

"Hope deferred makes the heart sick"

(Proverbs 13:12a)

The rent at the love nest went up and up again. We had a guest who became a permanent resident. (Remember the perky, random teenager from Niagara Falls? It's amazing how seemingly mere acquaintances become deep relationships.) So, it was time to look for a bigger nest. This served as a valuable lesson in, "When something looks too good to be true, it usually is."

The ad said, "Newly Renovated." It didn't say it was because sewage kept coming up through the drains or that the walls were so thin we could hear our neighbor's alarm clock go off. Every. Single. Morning! The local cats chose our front dirt patch as the neighborhood public facilities, and it stank! Besides all that—and there was plenty more, but I have a strong dislike for whining—the place had an icky feel. One evening, a police officer knocked on our door to inquire how long we had lived there, and we told him just a few weeks. When he said this address had been flagged as a "high incident" address, we were not surprised. He was responding to a call next door, and he said he would remove the flag because we were new. The five hundred dollars we were "saving" by living here didn't compensate for the bad atmosphere. We realized the importance of not making a decision based on price alone.

The months were passing, and every month I would find I was not pregnant. I would do a pregnancy test a day or two before my cycle date in hopes of seeing two lines, but it was always negative. At first, I would respond quite well, thinking, "Well, it may take a few months. Give it time." I tried a few tricks to help things along, like taking my temperature to determine optimal ovulation. I heard that by propping your legs up, gravity helps with the introduction of egg and sperm. That one kind of kills the afterglow, but I was becoming desperate. Each month's disappointment heaped on top of the one before, the temporary excitement of baby anticipation had evaporated, and a formidable dark cloud rolled in.

What exactly was the problem? I read all the information I could find on improving your chances to conceive, and all I really learned was that "just relax" was not the answer! It had become my most prevailing thought—an obsession. Why? Why was this not working? Burning tears streamed down my face as I looked at another negative test. I felt sick in the pit of my stomach, and fear began swirling over me. *"What if I can't get pregnant?"* I thought, *"Oh no... Not that, God. Please, no."*

That other voice with the impeccable timing and seething tone seized that opportunity to speak: "God is the one who gives babies. How could you think you would ever deserve this? Babies are for mothers, and let's face it, you are not mother material. What could you teach a child? How to be weak? How to be insecure? How to hide secrets? You certainly have lots of those, don't you? Remember who you are, and remember what you've done. You are lucky to be in God's good graces but don't think that qualifies you for a child."

I began to do something that put me on a truly slippery slope. I began doubting. I doubted I was good. Was I truly saved? I doubted God really loved me. I doubted my dream would come true. I began to despise the weak, pathetic reflection I saw in the mirror. This thought became a belief, *"What man could ever love the likes of you?"* Abysmal sadness returned, moved in, and brought a friend called insecurity.

So I began to fill the deep ache with food. The more pain I felt, the more I ate. The uglier I felt, the more I ate. Now I was overweight: proof that I was not lovely. I was convinced there was no way my husband could see me as beautiful either. This fortress I was building would not be complete without a welcome mat for jealousy, so she moved in and brought two sisters, criticism and suspicion. You would think the Cindy House of Strongholds was getting full, but there always seemed to be room for one more.

How did I manage that internal whirlpool while putting on the face of a happily married young lady? Well, try to keep up; it went like this: Every month, my cycle would start with heartbrokenness leading to self-pity. This would flow into a week of anger and self-loathing, throw in a few fits of rage, and accusing everyone else of being messed up. Then came desperation filled with negotiation and begging prayers. Loose threads of hope would have me grasping to make sense of it. Maybe this was all a matter of timing, a big mistake that God was not withholding because of my wretchedness. Four weeks later would bring another negative test result, and the cycle would repeat all over again! Phew, it's amazing my adrenal glands didn't crash, but I was resilient that way.

If I had a head-down desk job I might have managed to work better, but working with my clients, many of whom I saw weekly, it was playful banter to ask the newlywed, "How long till you'll be needing maternity leave?" When I walked past the baby department to get to the salon every day, the bassinets mocked me, and the frilly dresses dared me to come closer. These things made it difficult to put out of my mind. On the black days, I would call my husband from work crying and say, "I don't think I can finish my shift; the darkness is so bad." He would pray for me, talk to me kindly, and do all he could to lift my spirits like David's harp for Saul. Then, like Saul, the next day I would throw swords of accusation at him for not honoring me.

I would jealously challenge Lance's interactions with women. His strongest quality had always been loyalty, but that was no match for the critical thoughts that plagued my mind. I would see him speaking with a woman in a room filled with people and later drag him through the coals because of how it may "look" to others. I became the echo of the voice that tormented me. That was a difficult season for him. One time I asked him, "Is there any other job you could do besides being a pastor?" The disappointment in his eyes only solidified the feeling that I was not enough to make him happy. We were leaders in a church, we had friends, we had families who loved us, we had everything, but we had nothing!

Where was God in all this? What about the girl who had such vivid conversations with her Lord? In the Bible, we see that Satan had conversations with God about Job. Just because you talk to him doesn't mean you are close, and if you are close to him one day, it does not guarantee closeness in the future. If only I had kept talking and listening to him during that time. I was married to a pastor; I should have been the one helping others find their way, but I was the one who was lost.

It is intricate and precise how God weaves his plan for us even through our lack of listening and prideful actions. Lance had been working two jobs, and he wanted to be full-time at what he loved, so we thought it was time to live life instead of sitting around waiting for something to happen. God didn't seem to be directing us, and still, nothing was happening in the baby department. The old row house we were living in had no feelings of warmth or home. While out for a drive one night, we saw a huge lit-up sign advertising, "Show Homes–Condos–$1000 Gets You Started." (There was no mention of how much it takes to get you finished!) The "get you started" part really caught our eyes. We parked the car and walked in, heads held high like serious buyers. These were the very first floor plans I had ever seen! I had no comprehension of what square footage was. I heard "brand new" and "two bathrooms," and I was ready to sign. We felt so grown up. Yup, we were now taking charge! I'm sure there were angels snickering at how we thought we were being so spontaneous when they knew this meeting and the grand decision did not surprise God. That was it; we went out for a drive and bought our first house… just like that! Even though the move-in date was months away, the cool blast of spontaneity was exhilarating. Finally, it felt like we were leading, not being dragged along with no say-so what so ever.

5.

⌒

HOUSE OF HEALING

*""Through wisdom a house is built, and by understanding
it is established: And by knowledge the rooms are filled
with all precious and pleasant riches"*

(Proverbs 24:3, KJV)

Adults can get flashbacks of childhood that are triggered when an exact replica emotion is experienced. That's what happened when we moved into the brand-new condo. I was instantly eight years old on Christmas morning when I had the largest present under the tree, which clearly communicates favorite child, right? It was a brand-new dollhouse with three stories, each a different color, tiny furniture, and a miniature doll family. It was the most extravagant gift I had ever received. I hadn't thought of that dollhouse in twenty years, and it was refreshing to have such a happy memory. This home was new, and it was ours. Surely this was the sign of new beginnings.

Our newly purchased condo just happened to be a few blocks away from the new church where Lance had been hired. We had no idea of this at the time of the purchase. We thought we were taking control, but it was all in God's plan, not ours. The ministry was going well for Lance. He was the full-time youth pastor and had a wealth of creativity to meet the task.

My big life change was leaving the hair salon and finding a completely different career. I knew I would miss my regular clients, but the job was hard on the back and feet. I also wanted to leave with a good attitude. I had seen many stylists stay at it because it was all they knew, but they felt trapped and lost the joy.

I got a tip from my sister-in-law that a medical company was hiring. It is humorous how God works in and through misunderstandings. I confess I am completely weak in anything to do with blood, needles, and emergencies! I am the last person you want to be alone with if you suddenly require medical help. I panic. I get woozy. I'm not a rise-to-the-occasion girl. I know this because I have seen two people collapse. The first time, I stepped back and crouched low with my arms over my head. I think it was a way to prevent anyone from looking to me for leadership. The second time, a woman fainted, and I did what I had seen in the movies and slapped her face. Unfortunately, I wasn't aware when she regained consciousness and continued slapping. I did not even get so much as a "thank you" for saving her life.

I filled out the application and actually had an appointment for an interview for what I thought was a receptionist position. I did not have a ton of job interview experience, but I had enough to know I was rocking this one. There were two ladies interviewing me, and they were nodding their heads yes, leaning in, and smiling. You didn't have to be a mind reader to see they were pleased to meet me. I wondered if the lady at the reception desk was resigning or why they needed a second full-time employee for the small front area.

That thought was answered promptly as the lady who would be working directly with me said casually, "We will require that you learn to draw blood, but that will be the least needed of your tasks in working with the specimens."

"Speci... speci... blood! Oh... I am so, so sorry. This is a colossal misunderstanding. You see, I thought

I was applying for a reception job. I get nauseous at the thought of blood. Like right now I am feeling it rise… If I need my blood drawn, I have to lie down. I can't look, and I need the promise of a cookie if I don't cry. So, I am terribly sorry for wasting your time, but there is no way this could ever work."

The two interviewers enjoyed my honesty and cackled. One was dressed in scrubs, which was just now registering to my brain. They assured me they could teach anyone to process specimens. How desperate was this company?

I politely and slowly tried again. "I also have a strong aversion to unpleasant smells. What you are describing, the preparing of bodily fluids for testing, would have me heaving in the wastebasket. So I'm sure you don't want someone like me distracting the others."

The lady in the office suit now laughed louder than the one in scrubs. She cut into my explanation by announcing, "She's perfect. She will fit right in." If the continuous nodding was some kind of psychology to get me to agree, I was on to them.

I tried a different, firmer direction. "Even if I wanted to try and see if this could fit, I have committed to going on a mission trip with my husband's youth group for three weeks and couldn't possibly start before next month," thinking this would be the deal-breaker. They obviously wanted warm bodies today.

The business suit lady with the seniority, matter-of-factly stated, "Well, that settles it then. We will see you in a month. Have a great trip! And don't worry, Cindy, we supply masks to reduce the unpleasant smells."

Did that really happen? I wanted a change but not real-life experience in one of the world's worst jobs!

It all began very simply. I was confirming the spelling of names on the specimen-to-lab request sheet. Then I was steadily responsible for greater tasks. I did eventually learn how to draw blood—just one time, the requirement for me. I did it sitting down and looked away while the vial was filling with a wastebasket handy, just in case. I passed every new benchmark I was given, and within three years, I was the night supervisor! The only thing that had convinced me to show up for the first day of work was the incredible rate of pay and the benefits package. I knew I needed those with our plans for a baby.

The dream to have a baby morphed into the obsession to just get pregnant, and it still wasn't working. Finally, we decided to go to a doctor. I was not too up on medical advancements, but I was pretty sure they could give you a pill, and that bun would be in the oven within days.

We sat in a tiny sterile room and waited and waited. Surprisingly, I was not nervous. I was excited, which shows how unenlightened I was about my situation. Finally, the white coat man entered and began asking questions right out of the gate. Every answer we gave would result in a new paper handed to us, ordering a different medical test. The white coat man eventually looked up and said with a boring, institutional tone, "These tests will point us to the reasons why you two are infertile."

Whoa, just a minute there... Not only was that completely insensitive and rude—it was wrong. It had to be wrong. God, let it be wrong. Of all the self-loathing, awful names I had called myself over the years, and the list was lengthy, *infertile* was not one of them.

The doctor went on to say, "When you have been trying to conceive for more than a year, you fall into the infertile category, and you guys are closer to three. So, most likely, you will not be able to have children, but do the tests and we will see."

Numb. Numb is protection when you're in shock, so you don't feel the pain of a traumatic injury. We casually got up. I'm pretty sure we actually thanked him, and we walked out to our car as naturally as if we just bought a jug of milk at the corner store. There is nothing more awkward than two uncomfortable people trying to act nonchalantly. The space between us felt like a desert, a barren desert.

I cried every day following that appointment. It required all my energy to do the least of what needed to be done. My heart ached like it was full of shards of splintery glass. I grieved for someone I loved whose face I had never seen. They had died, and a part of me was with them.

What came next proves that Satan is evil. A worthy adversary would assume victory at that point, but he was just getting started. Lance is the only son of a rich family heritage; one of his great-grandfathers was a founder of Confederation for Canada. Lance had grown up hearing that he was the last one to carry on the family name: "You have to have a son." One day, I surfaced from my self-grief long enough to see the pain in my husband's eyes.

That's when Satan went for the kill: "You know, if he'd known you couldn't conceive, he never would have married you." Satan's mocking laugh made me tremble as I wondered how I could have been so blind. I knew Lance was sad at what the doctor said—chances are we won't have a baby—but he's really tortured because he's married to me; he's stuck. My lying enemy left me enough rope to figure the rest out.

I'm not sure it falls into the category of prayer, but talk to God I did. "God, how could you do this? You are so cruel. Lance must be sick to think he's stuck with me, but he would never divorce me. How could you allow me to ruin his life, too? I can handle you not wanting to give me a baby. I know I don't deserve it. I fooled myself thinking I could ever be a good Christian but have I now dragged him into *my* consequences?"

There were unspoken conversations hanging in the atmosphere between Lance and me as we mechanically went about our routines. A few times, I looked at him, willing him to truthfully answer my question: "Would you have married me if you knew?" I never had the courage to speak it.

My new job had transitioned into full-time night shifts, which made it smooth for cohabitating. After all,

I had no daytime responsibilities to worry about. The deep sadness eased to a constant ache of confusion, but at least it was livable. It became our new normal.

The church was bringing in a speaker, and the lead pastor asked Lance if he (we) could host him at our place. Lance came home and told me the "cool" news! Not to ask or to discuss, but to tell me! I was furious; the lead pastor had a five-bedroom house. Why are we the hosts? This was a horrible time to have a guest.

Lance went on to mention, "The speaker has dietary requests. He is a prophet, and he's currently fasting, so he's just eating vegetables."

"No, no, no... it's bad enough to have a stranger in our home, but even worse to have some weirdo who just takes one look at you and sees all your mess. Not to mention, I hate vegetables. I don't even know how to cook them." I completely lost the fight, and the next day we were on our way to meet Dennis Wiedrick, bring him back to the condo, and, I guess, feed him corn.

We sat outside the pastor's office on cheap metal folding chairs, waiting for the door to open. I began perspiring like a lawn sprinkler on pulse mode. I wondered if he would just throw out his words from God when he laid eyes on us or if he would need a day to figure us out. I was ready, still sweaty, but ready. He will probably say something like, "I'm surprised you two are married!"

To which the lights will come on, and Lance will think, "Yeah, why am I with her?"

The door handle turned, I took a deep breath, and we walked into the office to meet Mr. Scary. A broad man stood to greet us: rosy cheeks, white stubble beard, and smiling eyes. He was a hugger, embracing us both at the same time.

He stepped back, holding my left arm and Lance's right, and pronounced, "Oh my, you both have such a mantle of intercession on you. It's absolutely beautiful!"

Every cell in my body relaxed. The man was crackers; he couldn't see anything. I had no more gifting of prayer on me than I had the ability to dance the tango. Phew! Now I just had to feed him and get through the next few days.

Dennis was intriguing and very generous with his heart. He was full of compliments. It was interesting that he talked about God in a way that assumed we were on the same page as he was. He talked about how we were all sons and daughters and how God wasn't looking for hirelings. It sounded so normal the way he said it, but it felt like earth-shattering news. He explained the parable of the Unforgiving Debtor from Matthew 18 about a man who had been forgiven a massive debt by the king but then turned around and wouldn't forgive a fellow-servant of a pittance by comparison. Dennis explained what a debtors' prison was, that a whole family could be sold into labor until the debt was paid. Lance and I both understood that some of the heaviness we carried was due to unforgiveness and that debtors' prison pays wages until we released those we were offended with. After three days of microwaved mixed frozen vegetables, Dennis told us he felt the Lord was telling him to end his fast. (To think my cooking was so bad it made a prophet cave in worried me a little.) Dennis was staying in the city to do services in a different church, but his presence felt so comfortable to us, we invited him to stay longer. I knew he was a true prophet. I felt like one of the men on the road to Emmaus, who remarked, "Did our hearts not burn within us?"

Our last meal together was at a noisy burger restaurant. There was much commotion around us, so Dennis leaned in a little in his casual, unassuming way to present us with a random statement: "You both know, don't you... You did not choose each other. Your marriage was rooted in heaven." Extending his large hands toward us, he said, "God did the choosing long before you ever met." We smiled and nodded with appreciation. Inside I marveled at the revealing of my heart; the very fear I carried from the enemy's voice was silenced.

Because of opposite schedules, we didn't see much of each other during the week, so our weekends were enjoyable. After one Sunday service, an older man in a denim shirt with rolled-up sleeves and worn jeans who was very tall with a tan-weathered face and possibly the bluest eyes I have ever seen walked up to me, and as he began to speak, the strangest thing happened. He began to weep, not just tear up, but like the floodgates had opened. I picked out of his stammered words that he wanted to talk to me and Lance together.

I guided him by the elbow, grabbing a box of tissue on the way. "Lance," I whispered, "this interesting man wants to speak to us together!"

The next wave of the flood came, and through his

gentle voice and sobs, we heard, "You don't know me. I'm a farmer. I'm no one special, but I want to obey God, and he wants me to tell you you're going to have a baby." That was it, and if the words he spoke didn't grab my spirit's attention, the humility by which he spoke sure did.

We were quite shocked, not sterile-doctor-office-shocked, but we had only told our family of what the doctor said, so we sat there stunned. Tears filled our eyes as an invisible hammer chiseled away the icy distance between us. We left church that morning with something we did not have on the way in—hope.

We went for a long walk and the dam that had held back the honesty for so long broke. Yes, we both assured each other we would have still married the other if we had known; that was non-negotiable and a sweet relief.

We talked about adopting; we talked about traveling; we talked about getting healthy and losing weight; we began to dream again. I guess this is the part of my journey in which I can identify with Sarai from the Bible. Genesis 16:3 says it was ten years from the word of the Lord to when Sarai "took Hagar the Egyptian servant and gave her to Abram as a wife." Because I heard the word of the Lord, I thought it would happen soon.

I have wondered if everyone has a theme for their life, mostly because I have identified the theme of my life as "wait." So strong is this theme that I should wear a warning when shopping that says, "Don't stand behind me; I always choose the longest line." The waiting is not a curse because I have often felt it's the beginning of maturity, as this Scripture shows:

> Don't run from tests and hardships, brothers and sisters. As *difficult as they are, you will ultimately* find joy in them; if you embrace them, your faith will blossom under pressure and teach you true patience as you endure. *And true patience brought on by* endurance will equip you to complete the long journey and cross the finish line—mature, complete, and wanting nothing.
>
> James 1:2–4 (VOICE)

The testing of our faith continued. How I wish I had an enduring, blossoming tale to tell!

We waited, and nothing happened. We went through with all the testing from the stack of papers from the doctor, and nothing happened. We did our part (faith without works is dead!), and nothing happened. The medical results firmly stated it was my problem, then they firmly stated, no, it was Lance's problem. They bounced back and forth a few more times, all to say that we were definitely infertile, and we fell into the "unexplained" category. This was a very frustrating category to be in.

Like customers going through the express line with full carts, everyone around me became pregnant. You may think I am exaggerating, but even the cows in the fields started birthing when I showed up! Some ladies had the audacity to have two, even three, children! My irritation was akin to being at a social function with an extravagant buffet, and ladies were lining up to receive seconds when some of us hadn't had firsts yet! Me. What about me? I wanted to scream, "What about me!"

At first, I held very tightly to our message from God, and I would hold each new baby at church and think to myself, "Soon it will be you, girl. Get ready." But as year after year went by, I doubted. The book of James in the New Testament says: "Because the one who doubts is like a wave of the sea, blown and tossed by the wind" (James 1:6b). This is a very accurate description of where doubt led me.

There were many messages from God after the words from that kind, blue-eyed man. Every time I would feel the bottom falling out, God would send another message. There was one very interesting woman… Okay, I may as well just say it: she was a crazy prophetic lady unlike anyone I had ever met before, and we shared the same name. Lance and I were at an interfaith prayer service, praying for our city. The meeting was in a small, inner-city church, an area of town I wouldn't normally frequent. At the end of the service, there was an invitation for prayer ministry for the pastors who were present, so we went forward and stood in one of three lines. We were expecting a prayer of blessing over us, a prayer to better evangelize in our local church. The lady standing before us started by asking us if we had children. We said, "No," with our heads hung down.

She replied, "Are you sure?"

Wow, did we get in the wrong line up! "We are pretty sure we don't have children," we said, trying not to sound indignant.

"Oh." She seemed genuinely confused by our response. "It's just because I saw a picture of you two with a girl and a boy. Hmm..."

Hmm was right. Talk about pondering the possible symbolism of that one.

Each word would be an encouragement for a time, and then it would fade like the tossing of a wave back and forth.

I defaulted to what I had become very good at—slowly putting up walls. Exhausted by hurt, I stopped holding babies, I stopped going to baby showers, and I stopped going to church on Mother's Day. The more I isolated, the clearer one thing became: the familiar sound of my enemy's voice as he whispered, "The farmer was wrong. Maybe God was taunting you. Only a cruel person would do this to you. You have waited patiently; where is the baby?" It hurt so much. Proverbs says one of the four things that are never satisfied is a barren woman. How well I know that!

I checked the metal mailbox in the condo lobby and found a wad of flyers. I enjoyed building my grocery list by looking at the ads, so I sat down with paper, pen, and coffee. And there was a letter from our sponsor child. Those letters with crayon drawings were so sweet, and even though it wasn't an actual adoption, it felt like something. I knew right away it wasn't the usual letter. It was thinner and on plain white paper without the colorful border. It was a letter explaining that our sponsor child, whom we had for two years, chose to go with a different organization! Are you kidding me? Why not tattoo *rejected* on my forehead for everyone to see and get it over with. One of the neediest children in the world said, "No thanks. I pick someone else!" Maybe I was the last to know what everyone else could already see.

I told God in no uncertain terms that I couldn't take this anymore. It hurt too much to hope. I was getting close to forty years old, and in the fertility world, that was ancient. In a matter-of-fact tone I had learned from somewhere, I laid out my rules for God—I will do my best to be a good person, but I'm not talking to you about this anymore. In fact, I don't want you talking to me about it either. Don't send one more person with a baby-message. I did not listen for a response. I closed a door and carried on. *Epic fail* is defined by *Urban Dictionary* as "complete and total failure when success should have been reasonably easy to attain." That prayer to God was an epic fail! What I needed most were solace and courage. If only I had waited and listened as it says in Isaiah: "Yet those who wait for the

Lord will gain new strength; they will mount up with wings like eagles, they will run and not be tired, they will walk and not become weary" (Isaiah 40:3, NASB). I could have renewed my strength, and I would have unearthed what I so yearned for: a path to healing. But I took the highway to more pain.

We all have a God vacuum inside us—that was the way they described it when I was a teen—and if you didn't fill it with God, it was inevitable that you would try to satisfy the emptiness with something else. So, in the quest to fill the vacuum, we traveled to Disneyland, Disney cruises, the Dominican Republic. There was one wistful moment on the deck of the Disney cruise ship when I thought that if we ever did have children, I'd sure want to bring them here. We got cats, but one of them died from kidney disease, which was more confirmation that life was cruel. We joined a gym and went a lot; busy people don't have time to wallow in self-pity. All these ventures in themselves were not bad, but they were unsuccessful in stopping the pain and filling the void.

Nearly eight years passed from when we had started trying to conceive, and, as it happened, it was another unsuspecting Sunday morning. (My experience seems to be that God is extra busy on Sundays.) I walked into the church right on time because if I were early, that would mean socializing with people. I was feeling strong and in control. There was a slight edge of anger, but compared to pitiful weakness, I felt like I was winning. I loved the way I looked. Did I mention I had joined a gym? (Don't cheer yet. I was actually skinny for only two weeks.) With three promotions at my job, I was successful. My emotions were coolly tucked away where one could only see the tight-lipped smile on my face. I was proud that I found a working formula. I had figured it out, and I could live like this forever. In fact, I had been successful for almost a year. No longer did I feel like a teetering glass about to spill. I wonder, did angels nudge each other and smile at how clever I thought I was? Did they get a good seat to watch what happened next?

As I was taking my usual seat that Sunday morning, I heard it. It was unmistakable, and my stomach started to turn. No way! There is only one person who whispers my name in that way, and I would recognize that voice anywhere: "Cindy." Spoken as a tender invitation, reminding me he never gives up. Just because he had been quiet did not mean that he had left.

My heart immediately wrenched. I was so angry. I was doing so well, but his voice could ruin everything. Venomously, I spewed my response to him much braver than I felt: "What do you want."

He never beats around the bush, and he can say more in three words than humans can in volumes of books. Without missing a beat, he coaxed, "Hold a baby."

I was utterly defenseless as he revealed the moment I had closed my heart. I felt like the rich young ruler who had been told to sell everything. He asked me to do the hardest and most humbling task. I weakly protested, "I can't do that."

There was no response. It was then and there that I found there was something far worse than physical barrenness—a crushed spirit, who can bear? I knew that through the revelation of his words that the place to start was the very place I had shut down. All my strength dissipated like a falling balloon, deflated. I craved for his presence, even his correction was soothing, and I knew, for me, what the cost of living in his presence would be.

I looked around the sanctuary. All eyes were facing the front as the pastor was coming to the close of his message. I cannot recall one word he spoke that day. My searching fell on the newest born in our church, "Oh, Lord, will you crush my heart here today?"

Like warm, gentle ripples on hot sand, a Scripture washed over me: "'For I know the plans I have for you,' declares the Lord, 'Plans to prosper you and not to harm you, plans to give you hope and a future'" (Jeremiah 29:11). And I chose to give God a chance to heal me through obeying him. After all, I had tried everything else.

After the service, I quietly slipped beside the young mom; she looked little more than a child herself. She was a vision of a gentle heart. God was so gracious to afford me privacy as everyone else seemed to be caught up in pockets of conversation. "Can I hold your baby?" I squeezed out the words, trying to sound as nonchalant as possible but failing miserably.

"Oh, sure," she gushed. She was pleased to have an admirer of her most precious treasure, and the sleeping bundle was in my arms. I did it! The baby stirred and calmly opened her dark little eyes. She looked right at me, and I felt like she knew all my secrets. Then I felt a wave of pure grace as my heart melted at the wonder I held. I opened my heart completely, and all the pain poured out. How cleansing it is to be forgiven! Oh, how I missed being free! The unsuspecting mother thought I was overcome by her baby's beauty, and, in part, I was.

God's voice whispered again, "What do you want, Cindy?"

"This," I said with a depth of honesty that surprised me "I want to hold my baby; I want to feel and hear you every day; I want a crazy, unbelievable marriage; I want it all. I want to be whole." I looked up to see Lance watching me from a few feet away—that look communicated more than one thousand conversations.

I left church that morning one hundred pounds lighter, and no one in the congregation was the wiser. Never underestimate God's ability to work on a heart even when nothing shows from the outside. I was reminded of the story of Hannah in 1 Samuel. Her husband would ask, "Don't I mean more to you than ten sons?" (1 Samuel 1:8). And I finally understood the God vacuum; nothing can satisfy your heart but God.

It was as if I had been invited to dance. God gave the invitation, I responded yes, and we began to move together. It no longer felt like a riddle to be deciphered but a dance, a beautiful, moving-together dance. The identity of *rejected* fell away, and we just focused on things that seemed productive. We were led to a season of healing. At every opportunity, we received prayer. Person after person had words of encouragement, Scriptures of promise, and confirmations of what we knew in our hearts. We learned about spiritual birthright and thought maybe it was a spiritual block, not a physical one. We renounced, repented, took authority, blessed, and laid hands on everything possible. We came to a place where we realized the spiritual discovery was done. It was not a waste of time; we were sowing seeds for a future harvest, and we learned so much about prayer. But there comes the point when you've done the work, and you have to trust and wait.

We did look into adoption because Lance's mom was adopted, and it seemed like a sensible fit. I brought home a pile of brochures, excited to dive into the ocean of information. The brochures were anticlimactic. We agreed; we both felt a solid closed door. Sometimes "No" is a relief because there is no room for doubt. Adoption is in God's heart; it just wasn't his plan for us.

This time waiting was easy, and as in *The Message* version of Romans, chapter 8, we became "enlarged in the waiting." I joined a running club, and although I was a far cry from Eric Liddell, I did feel God's pleasure when I ran. The distinct presence of the Holy Spirit was so intense when I would go for a run. I would feel an increased faith to pray for others, a knowledge of his heart and his ways. I was so blessed to experience his presence daily. Finally, I was strong spiritually and physically.

It was during a run that prayer simply rolled out of my heart. I was running over a bridge. I'm a bit nervous about heights, so I was concentrating on not looking over the edge beside me. Between heavy breaths, I prayed, "God, if I never have a baby, it's okay. I don't feel empty *anymore*." It was a thought-prayer, but it opened a door for two dear friends to return. Peace and joy were in the house; life was good.

6.

HOUSE OF
HAPPINESS

*The Spirit of God is arousing us within. We're also feeling
the birth pangs. These sterile and barren bodies of ours
are yearning for full deliverance. That is why waiting does
not diminish us any more than waiting diminishes a pregnant mother. We are enlarged in the waiting. We, of course,
don't see what is enlarging us. But the longer we wait, the
larger we become, and the more joyful our expectancy.*

Romans 8:23–25 (MSG)

Nadine, Lance's younger sister, wanted to get into
the housing market, and our little condo was po-
sitioned to turn a good profit. We found a great location where they were building duplexes; wouldn't it be
fun to be next-door neighbors! This would be a place
to settle in. We were loving life, and this new house
would have a lot more room when needed. It had a ga-

rage. No more lugging groceries up to the third floor. This was a family home, and it sure felt like God was enlarging the nest.

I had stopped playing church and actually started being the church. I loved to help out in any way. (I even helped a family with a lice problem—this had to be God!) I loved helping Lance and encouraging others. I especially enjoyed ministering to women who, like me… well, like I used to be… were paralyzed by lies. Satan has imprisoned many women with the lie unworthy. That will always be Satan's goal: to convince the beloved that they are not!

Our dear friend Dennis was back in town for a conference, and we were delighted to go to the service just to see him. He had been so instrumental in revealing the father heart of God; he would always be dear to us. Dennis asked Lance if we would give his friend a ride back to the hotel after the service. Lance was happy to oblige. Dennis' friend was Bob Jones, one of the speakers. He was an older man, and although Lance and I had no prior knowledge of him, he was a well-known American prophet.

Dennis called Lance aside and said, "Lance, I told Bob that I would like him to ask God for an answer to any question you want to ask him." He then asked, "Why don't you ask him about you and Cindy getting pregnant." This was very strange to Lance. He told me what Dennis said and left to escort the nice older man and his wife to the car.

I was excited. I didn't know much about Bob Jones, but I did feel like God was somehow in this. The four of us were in the car, and Lance said, "So, how are you doing tonight?"

Inside, I'm banging my head: "No… what if that's your question!"

Lance went on to explain that we had been trying to conceive for nine years and how Dennis recommended we ask him about that.

Bob very calmly said, "Put your hand on your wife's left side, pray for her, and she will be healed."

Lance and I thought that was nice of him, but at that point, we had been told it was likely Lance who hindered conceiving. So, Lance said, "Actually, the doctors think it's me, not my wife."

Bob repeated, "Pray for her. She will be healed."

This was like watching a tennis match going back and forth.

Finally, Bob said a little more firmly, "Don't worry. You have enough to get the job done. Just pray for your wife."

It was not a warm, fuzzy parting. We never exchanged addresses for Christmas cards. It was brief and weird. We knew one thing for sure: if God was in this, we had to obey. As soon as we were alone in the car, Lance reached over and put his hand on my left side. I felt a heat deep inside my body, and I began to laugh—not that it was funny, but from that deep place, a bubbling of joy began to pour out of me. I was laughing, and tears were also flowing. I don't know what happened, but something changed.

Lance was driving with one eye on the road and one eye on me. We had to go pick up another couple back at the church to give them a ride home. I love this about Lance—although he was not laughing with me, he allowed whatever was happening in me to have its completion. We picked up the next couple, and when they were puzzled by my laughter, he just said, "This is my wife. She's not usually like this." I could have stopped. I know I could have, but why would I want to? I felt years of sorrow wash away.

I wondered if that would be a prayer of healing for

us to conceive. We had talked about our doctor's recommendation of *in vitro* fertility treatment. I had a stack of brochures that made my head swirl. I did not want to go against God and take this into our own hands. Would this be the ultimate betrayal of my Lord to go to a doctor when he could so easily open my womb? We prayed together, and we asked our dear friend Dennis if he thought pursuing medical help would be a faithless mistake.

He was so genuine when he responded with a question: "Would it be wrong for a farmer to put fertilizer on his field?"

I blurted my reply, "But I don't want an Ishmael!"

His response sobered me, "Cindy, you're not Sarah!"

He was right. Lance and I were on our own journey, so we committed to continue walking it until God closed the door. The brochures were not made to build up false hope; there was a lot of medical terminology and lists of drug side-effects. How was one supposed to navigate the cost with all the different possibilities of how your procedure would go? One thing was certain: this would not be cheap. We booked an appointment. We would go to the IVF clinic three hours away in Calgary.

Lance had been away at a youth camp for a week, and when he returned and settled in, he held out a small business card to me.

I asked, "What's this?"

"A pastor approached me at the camp. He invited us to join their staff in Calgary."

"No, no, no!" I screamed in my head. Everything is perfect here; everything is perfect now. God would never ask us to leave a place where we are being so fruitful, would He? "What did you say?" I asked with a tone of caution.

He had been studying me to read my response.

"I said no. As much as I've always wanted to live in a bigger city, and the offer was quite generous, I can't see us leaving here now."

I let out the biggest relief sigh, "I know, right! Phew, that was a little scary."

I comforted myself with the thought that God doesn't just uproot people to put them somewhere else; that would not be his way. But he said, "Cindy, this is exactly my way. Remember the early church? It would not have grown if they had all stayed together in one place. You and Lance need to grow, and there are those whom you will help in the growth of their lives. As the heavens are higher than the earth, so are my ways higher than your ways."

I hate change. "I finally feel whole; are you certain, Lord?"

"Cindy, I am so glad you can experience my joy, but, my darling, you are not yet whole. For what is coming, you have to move. You need to fix your gaze on me because I am the only one who never changes."

"Father, I will not trade my place in your heart for anything ever again, so I yield to your will completely." I felt a wave of peace and smiled to myself as I thought, *I wonder if it rattles the enemy to see the old plans not working on me, to see me dive deeper into my Lord's heart instead of running away, still weak but stronger than I've ever been before.*

My greatest joy had become walking with ladies through the hindrances in their lives. Most of my time was spent in small groups or on walks, just encouraging or praying with gals. I didn't have training or schooling, but on hearing someone's story, I could feel the Father's heart for them. I would speak his love and truth over them. Truth really does set a person free. It was exhilarating to watch.

One of the ladies I spent time with gave me a card to say thank you. As I opened the plain white envelope, the picture on the front of the card captured me. It was a young shepherdess holding a little lamb. Funny how God will use such seemingly insignificant moments and components to trumpet his secret messages to us. That is God's way: beauty from ashes, humans from dirt, the more common the vessel, the brighter he shines.

Our little church was not the sort you would see on TV or that would host a big event. We were a unique bunch of ragamuffins who gathered in one place. What others would call misfits, we found to be a loving community. We wanted to host a ladies' retreat. This would be a big step for us to plan, and we knew we better pray it through first.

The rain was falling. Big drops that splattered when they hit the surface, the kind of rain that makes even adults tip their heads back and open their mouths to try and catch a drop. Our small group of ladies ran inside the church like giggling schoolgirls. We had planned who the speaker would be, made a list of potential locations, and as we tried to guess the possible number of ladies attending, we thought it was a good time to stop and pray.

My friend Sharon prayed that all the ladies would feel welcome to attend.

"Yes," I agreed.

Sharon continued, "Lord, you are the God of Abraham, Isaac, and Jacob. We want all the generations to be there."

Then, as unsuspecting as that white envelope, I heard him say, "Cindy, I am also the God of Sarah, Rebekah, and Rachel."

I nearly fell off my chair. I knew two things for sure: God was talking to me, and I knew he was not talking about the ladies' retreat. I knew Sarah (Abraham's wife) and Rachel (Jacob's wife) were barren, but Rebekah? I wasn't sure. So as soon as I got home, I opened my Bible and found her story. There it was in Genesis: "And Isaac prayed to the Lord for his wife, because she was barren. And the Lord granted his prayer, and Rebekah his wife conceived" (Genesis 25:21, ESV). Wow, my faith grew ten sizes that day. I just knew he was saying to me, "It's reality, and it's close." It was like money in the bank. Hope gave way to anticipation, and I walked around with the silliest grin on my face like I had this colossal secret. It felt that done.

Lance and I both felt a strong confirmation that we were indeed supposed to move to the new church. Next came the hard task of saying goodbye. How do you stand in front of people who have loved you so well, who, like family, have cried, prayed, and laughed with you through thick and thin? It seemed to be the strangest time to leave. I had always imagined celebrating a baby with these dear friends.

We made a trip to Calgary to meet the staff of the new church and spy out the land. We would be moving in a few weeks. Calgary is a beautiful city; the Rocky Mountains are only an hour away. Lance was excited for this new challenge. God was leading him in this season to spread his wings. We also had a doctor's appointment in Calgary that had been planned quite sometime before. We had moved from family doctor to fertility specialist.

The three-hour drive home felt like minutes as I reminisced the journey thus far. God was reminding me of his faithful heart through it all. Then I thought back to the appointment with Dr. Greening and the pictures of all those babies. I was so sure this doctor would check me out and say, "Guess what, you crazy kids, you are already pregnant!" So you can imagine how anticlimactic it was to actually hear, "Too bad you waited so long." Apparently, in the medical world, forty is not the new twenty, it's "your ovaries look old, very old." Initially, that fertility clinic appointment was not what I anticipated, but I was no longer the easily wounded target I used to be. It was a world of difference to be confident of the Lord's love, to see through his eyes instead of living like a victim who fearfully ran away.

One of the last things Dr. Greening said at that appointment was, "We don't make promises."

"No, you don't," I thought, *"but I know someone who has."* I just couldn't figure out why this fertility clinic would have anything to do with it. I didn't want to dishonor God and his way, but I had come to learn that when your heart is in the right place, God's ability to direct you is so much greater than your ability to miss him. I knew how I wanted my story to go. I wanted to say that nine months to the day after reading about Rebekah, I had a baby. But you don't always get to choose how your story goes—sometimes you just get to choose what kind of person you will be in it.

My biggest turmoil was wondering if there was a chance I was pushing my own agenda. It seemed that God was opening this door, but I wanted to know from him for certain. I did not want to come this far and blow it by not trusting God for a few more days, months, or years if needed. I would not trade what I held in my heart for what I could hold in my arms.

We began packing and said our gut-wrenching goodbyes. Passing by the kitchen patio windows, the brightness of the sun pouring through the glass enticed me to go look outside because, literally moments before, it had been pouring. I looked out to see the most brilliant, striking rainbow I had ever seen in my life. Enjoying the masterpiece, I stood a while and let my Lord's presence warm my heart and soul. A Scripture washed over me: "God's way is perfect. All of the Lord's promises prove true. He is a shield for all who look to him for protection" (Psalm 18:30, NLT).

Later that day, I talked to Sharon on the phone and asked, "Did you see that rainbow today?"

"Yes," she said, "and the unusual thing about it was that it was in the west. They are usually in the east."

I pondered in my heart, "God are you telling me your promise for me will come from a different direction than normal?" (As I write this, God has again allowed it to rain. I smile at his unabashed extravagance.)

I knew we were to keep walking through the IVF doctor's door for now because he did not give us a sure no, like the no we felt when considering adoption, although it was a challenge to my convictions. When I resigned from my job, I found that the company benefit savings account had accumulated enough to cover a large portion of the medical treatment cost. I still wasn't all in. Though I was grateful for the money, I whispered, "But Lord, I know you could speak the word, and it would be done."

The procedure was *in vitro* fertilization—IVF. The egg is removed from the female's ovaries, fertilized outside of the body with the man's sperm, and placed back in the female's uterus with the hope of establishing a successful pregnancy. I was reminded of Dennis's encouragement to us that this was like a farmer putting fertilizer on a field, and that would not be wrong. We would just be improving the chances of the best harvest possible. It was a nice picture and spoken with love, but was I now testing God's patience by not accepting it? I knew I still had time for God to confirm or cancel this. I was not opposed to an angelic visitation.

Well, some of the joys of preparing for the big implant day involved pills, lots of pills (I hate swallowing pills), and injections. (Remember, I also hate needles. I hate them more than swallowing pills!) The injections were every day for about ten days before the implanting. The injections were administered by my husband: not cool or romantic. Of all the ways I dreamed of getting pregnant, this was never one of them. It felt humiliating, and the needles made me cry. Of course, the fact that I was being pumped full of hormones probably didn't help. We would go to the clinic every couple of days to check on how many eggs were growing. They seemed to want enough to populate a new planet. The odds of having viable eggs were low, so they wanted to produce as many as they felt was safe to have the best chance. It was a lonely experience. It wasn't something any of my friends had gone through, so it wasn't like planning a bridal or baby shower where you call up a girlfriend and chat about the details. I knew one person who would have been able to relate. I learned that Lesley Brown was the first woman to have a successful birth from IVF in 1978. (She passed away in June 2012.) I just bet she never looked back and lamented that there was no one else who could share the exact same experience. I was more worried about being akin to the probable hundreds of unnamed women before her who were unsuccessful.

The morning of the final procedure had arrived, and there I sat on a couch with a cup of coffee and my Bible on my lap. I have never needed to hear from God like that morning. I was excited but still so fearful that I may be dishonoring God. I did not want to birth an Ishmael. I think that's where we get hung up as modern Christians, thinking that taking medication is somehow a disgraceful lack of faith. So, I prayed in desperation, "Lord, I'm scared. I just want you to do it. In my heart, it feels like I'm not trusting you. I want to trust you. Please, Lord, show me today if this is not your way."

"Cindy, read your Bible."

I looked down to where my Bible was opened on my lap. It was the book of John, chapter 9. I read about a man who was born blind, and Jesus healed him by spitting in the dirt, making mud, and putting it on his eyes.

The Lord spoke so clearly to me, "Cindy, do you know why I used mud on his eyes to heal him?"

"No," I answered. "Why did you?"

Then he asked me, "Do you think the man who could now see cared? Do you think when he could see the trees and the faces of those he loved for the first time, he was ashamed of the mud on him?"

I answered, "No, I don't think it mattered at all."

Every restraint fell away at his next words: "That's what I do. I turn ashes into beauty, shame into honor, and show the barren she has always been my beloved. When you hold your baby for the first time, you will not care if the conception was natural or with treatment."

With the only opinion that mattered now completely settled, I readied for the appointment with huge expectancy.

The disciples asked Jesus, "Why was the man blind? Was it his sin or his parents?"

Jesus answered the why, "This happened so the power of God could be seen in him."

I smiled as I thought of the enemy who tried to steal this moment from me, and with renewed courage, I thought, "Here's mud in your eye!"

So, it was weird and fascinating how the whole implantation deal went down. I was in a small room on a hospital bed. The room was dimly lit, and at first, I thought the low light was supposed to be tranquil, but it was to enable us to see the TV screen above to watch the whole procedure. Amazingly, we saw a long, needle-like instrument slowly insert and then release eggs into my uterus. Now it was time to wait and see if any would implant in the lining and if the lining would accept and thicken to grow the cute little embryo into a full-term baby. It all came down to that—it didn't strike me as medically fascinating, just simplistically fascinating.

In three weeks, we would do a home pregnancy test and call the clinic so they could add the result to our file and their statistics. The moving date was upon us, and we were quite busy with packing and visits to enjoy one last time before we left. The ladies retreat we had been planning the year before was happening that weekend, and I would know when I got home if the procedure was successful. As much as I tried to be spiritual, my mind was utterly consumed with was I or was I not pregnant? One minute I was in faith: "I believe I am." The next minute I would be a martyr: "Lord, if I am not, I trust you and your timing." My two closest friends, Sharon and Betty, kept smiling at me with raised eyebrows all through the weekend as if to say, "We're already celebrating!" It was a fantastic retreat, the ladies were blessed, and the goodness of God felt full circle.

I walked up the few steps to our house, knowing the first thing I would do and wondering if Lance was home or at the office. The butterflies in my stomach were worse than ever before; the prom and my wedding day did not come close.

I was startled when the door opened as I reached for the knob. I looked up to see Lance. "Hi" was all he said. He grabbed my wrist and proceeded to pull me inside and up the stairs.

"What are you doing?" I asked, totally bewildered.

Determined, he did not respond. He opened the bathroom door and pointed to the counter. I looked at a pregnancy stick ready to go. I exhaled with a fake laugh, and in that second, I thought of how many times I had done this before, and every single time the result had been negative. I looked back at my husband, whose face always gets flushed when he's intense, and it was flushed now.

His eyes held mine, and I saw in him a depth of

vulnerability that I had never seen before. "Here we go." That one minute felt like three days! Our identity hung in the balance. "Look now," he said.

I trembled the words: "I can't. You look and tell me."

"Two lines, Cin. That means positive, right?"

I am sure the scream that came out of my mouth shook the heavens. We laughed, and we bawled like a geyser of joy. Oh, death, where is your sting? The presence of an empty tomb filled that bedroom. The tears washed away all the scorn, all the pain, and I imagine at that moment I had a taste of what heaven must feel like.

Our parting from our home, city, and church was bittersweet. Our church family had carried the same hope with us for years, and this was just as much their victory. We got to share the pregnancy news, but it was painful to think we wouldn't be with them for the birth of this baby. But we knew we were following more than our hearts. We were following our king, our dream giver.

We were ready for our new life, new city, and a new job. My heart was as full as the moving truck—

not room for one more thing. I sat on the floor, looking around and feeling so undeserving of all the love and of the life now growing inside of me. As I pondered all that had happened, it just kind of spilled out: "Why do you love me?" I needed to know. It was not a prayer or a thought. There was a thread of suspicion rising up like a warning alarm, alerting me that this did not add up. "Why do you love me?" I repeated. "What's in it for you? Cindy, who is so unfaithful, so distracted, always promises way more than she can deliver. I don't even see potential that could be of use to you. Why? Why do you love dirt?"

He so gently but resolutely responded, "Not just dirt, dirt with my spirit in it. I made you. You did not just happen. I planned and designed you. I knit you. I am in you. You have my DNA. When I look in your eyes, I see my eyes. When a mother holds her baby for the first time, sees the life that was once inside her, and then, minutes later, holds that baby in her arms—she does not need a return for her affection. Her reward is the moment her heart beholds sacred love. For now, you will have to trust my words, but you will see."

7.

HOUSE OF
HARVEST

*"Wishes that come true are like eating fruit from the tree of
life"*

(Proverbs 13:12b, NCV)

We were so excited to go to our first ultrasound. We kept going back and forth about whether we wanted to find out the gender or not.

"Let's keep it a surprise," Lance coaxed.

I negotiated, "But I want to be prepared, and it's already real. I want to know this baby as a person."

Lance countered, "Maybe we should find out and not tell anyone else?"

Yes! We had the solution: we could know and still have a secret to reveal.

What a wonder to see a living life inside my body!

The swooshing around, kicking and stretching arms out like there was not enough space in there! It even had the hiccups. Adorable! This little embryo was coming along beautifully.

The technician was a kind lady who, although she had probably done this a thousand times, really made us feel special. "So, would you like to know?"

We looked at each other and unanimously replied, "Yes!"

She said, "Well, when it's a boy, it's pretty obvious. Keep in mind, it's a bit early to tell, but I would say, the high nineties, you've got a little girl."

Lance responded with, "Woot, woot!"

I had a big smile and welled up with tears. Surprisingly, I had a dreadful thought, *"How will I ever protect her?"* But I tried to shake it off and join Lance in the jubilation of the moment.

The ride home was obviously filled with the baby names discussion. This now became the heaviest decision a person could ever make. How do you choose an identity for someone you haven't met yet?

Due to a lack of abundant finances, God was pretty much on the hook to find us a home. We had left a modest duplex that was new but sold too early to make a profit, so we believed God would work this out. God provided a friend to stay with while we waited to find our place.

As we were considering our options, we were introduced to a business owner, a builder. This man, without ever talking to us before, wanted to extend an incredible offer to us because we were pastors. He said, "I believe God has blessed me, so I can, in turn, bless others. I want to build you a brand-new home at a reduced price, so you can get in the market. And in a few years, you can turn a profit." This was so hard to comprehend that I would swear the man was an angel, but he had a lifetime of back story, so he had to be human! We were so grateful for this man's generous and obedient heart, and just a few months later, we were in our very own brand-new first single-dwelling house! Consistently, for us, when God leads the way, he clears the way, reminding me that, "God can do anything, you know—far more than you could ever imagine or guess or request in your wildest dreams!" (Ephesians 3:20, MSG).

The curtains were hung; everything was in its place; there was nothing left to do except wait for the big day. With Lance deep in his new job and being in a new city, I thought it was the new quiet that made me feel blue. I walked, prayed, and baked, but I could not shake it. I didn't want to even bring it up to Lance. How dare I? Everywhere my eyes looked, I saw the blessings of my Lord. I would have to be the most selfish girl in the world to now say, "Wow, I know everything is nearly perfect, but I can't seem to shake this sadness." I couldn't even pray about it. Why did I feel guilty?

I decided to casually mention it to Lance in a way that sounded like even I thought I was crazy. Maybe if I just got it out, that would be the cure. That evening, the casual conversation I planned was the most impossible thing to bring up. The excuses in my mind were endless. Finally, I just stated, "I have something to tell you."

He looked at me and waited.

"Well...the thing is...that..." Why was this so hard? I was now ashamed of my inability to form a complete sentence.

"What's up? Are we okay?" He had not a clue what was inside me. I had to be honest; he was not a mind reader.

"Lance, I have been having that darkness over me again. I can't pray it away. I feel guilty because I should be so happy, and I am, but I can't shake this."

"Why do you think you're struggling?" His wheels were turning. I knew he was in fixer mode: If I missed my parents, he would say to go for a visit. If I said I was isolated, he'd suggest ways to get out and connect.

I had to be clear. "Since I heard that we were having a girl, I have been fearful that something bad could happen to her. You can't tell by looking at people who is dangerous or safe. How will we ever protect her?" At that point, hot tears were dripping from my chin.

His cheeks and forehead were red. He isn't a man who expresses emotions, but he does feel deeply. He was angry at someone who still had a measure of power over me. He was frustrated that there was no easy fix to this pain. He took both my hands and simply prayed, "God, we need you. We don't want the joy of this season to be stolen. Help my wife; help me." As he lifted his head, he remembered that, just this week, a new person came on staff at the church, a certified counselor. "Cindy, you should go see this guy. Maybe he can help?"

I was willing to do whatever it took to be done with

this once and for all. I went to meet with the counselor, hoping that with one magical conversation, I would be back to normal. He asked a few basic discovery questions: "What brings you here? How long have you felt this way? Do you know what could have triggered this?" That's where he stopped and really looked at me. When I told him I struggled with the fear that my little girl could possibly be violated, he said, "You've never dealt with what happened to you, have you?"

I explained, "I thought moving on was dealing with it."

Why is nothing ever easy or quick in my life? That's how I felt when he said, "Cindy, this will take a while, but if you're willing to do the work, you can be free of this forever."

There is nothing fun about looking at the pain in your life. Every Tuesday was a hard day. I was a good patient; I did all my homework. I had to read books, journal, and make a plan of what raising a child in a healthy and safe environment would look like. The counseling was working. I wasn't struggling with fear. I thought I was near my last appointment when he dropped a bomb: "This week's homework is that I want you to call or write your parents and ask them what would have happened if you told them when you were a girl about the sexual abuse." I couldn't tell my parents when I was a child, and I felt no more courageous to do so now.

The disappointment drove me to confront God. "God, is this really necessary? Why is it the most difficult request what you always seem to require of me?"

There was no response from God. I knew he wasn't going to negotiate with me; it was in my hands if I wanted to follow through or not.

I decided to call my mom, one of the strongest women I know. She is the third oldest of fifteen children: there was no nonsense, no whining; it was, get the job done and do it better than best. I picked up the phone to tell my tough-as-nails mom that I felt so weak.

I hung up the phone in awe of the workings of God in how the conversation went. She was surprised I was in counseling. When I told her we were covering things from childhood and what specifically that entailed, her responses restored value to my soul. She told me that I was raised to be polite and respect adults. I was raised in a time where no one talked about such things. She understood it would be hard for me to trust after those experiences, and before we hung up, she told me I was beautiful, and she was proud of me. I knew I was loved.

One week later I received a letter from my father,

My dear, sweet Cindy,

Now that you're expecting a little girl of your own, you know something of the joy your mom and I experienced when God gave you to us. I have always been so proud of you, and the fact that you are the spitting image of your mom makes you extra special. Only a father can understand how special that love for his daughter is. I have great memories of your childhood: the fun, the laughter, and the joy you brought into our lives.

When Mom shared with me what happened to you as a child and later as a teenager, I felt so hurt and sorry that this could have happened to my little girl. Mom asked what I would have done if I had known back then, twenty years ago. I would have reported him to the police. Thirty years ago, I wasn't as sanctified as I am now, so I probably would have taken some physical action as well.

I wish you had told us when it happened. Your mom and I would have been there for you, helped you get the help and healing you needed, and made certain that it would never happen again. Cindy, you are so precious to me, and I am so sorry that I could not see that you were in danger while you were in my care.

I am glad you are in counseling now. Let the Lord guide you in what action to take. Your mom and I are with you. Now that you know how easily these things can happen, prepare and train your child as soon as they can understand. We need to pray for our family every day.

All my love,
Your dad

Any threads of shame were washed away with the flood of tears upon reading that letter. I was no longer embarrassed; I was humbled by grace. From that day on, it no longer had power over me.

Like opening night on Broadway, the big day arrived. The pains grew in intensity, and I knew this was the real thing. I had previously discussed the options of natural birth, but a few hours after arriving at the hospital, I was willing to trade a kidney for an epidural.

It was a long delivery, and finally, the doctor said, "It's a girl!"

My heart's response surprised me, "I always wanted a girl. Oh, Lord, thank you, thank you! She's here." My heart overflowed with joy and praise.

My Lord softly gave a promise, "Cindy, I will walk close to her."

When she finally appeared, she came out talking! Her sounds were squeaks, ohs, ah, and aahs.

The doctor even remarked, "They don't usually do that!"

She was a beautiful wonder. Later we brought home one of the most celebrated baby girls this world has ever seen.

We were able to have a blessing party for our baby girl with our former congregation, which was more than celebration, it was victory. There were hours of blessings spoken over her. It was so tender to hear a blessing from the farmer, who was the first person to give us a message of hope. It truly felt full circle. McKenzie Nicole remains our child of promise. She came out talking and has not stopped to this day. I say, "I bet my living will she will be a lawyer!" Whatever God has for her will be big because she will not settle for anything less.

When God does such radical changes in your life and heart, you can get a sense of "Phew, I've arrived." I began to feel a certitude that I knew the rest of the story, and now I just needed to let it happen. I should have never assumed I knew the outcome. The ways of God will always be higher than the ways of humans.

Jumping into the "ever after" part of our story: we got involved in the community, made friends with our neighbors, and there was work. Working with the youth was a steeper learning curve. We thought we knew that ministry, but we didn't consider how the economy changes the spiritual temperature. Although we had worked with youth for over seven years, it was different here.

In Edmonton, we found poverty and single-parent families struggling with rejection, so the yearning for a father figure was great and impossible to fill. Continually we tried to help the youth to see God as their father and source. But in Calgary, it was difficult to find the need. These were middle- and upper-class, affluent families. There seemed to be no way to open their spiritual eyes to their need for a Savior. Lance prayed about this dilemma and felt the Lord leading him to take the kids on a mission trip to gain a different perspective. This was a great eye-opener. After the mission trip to Ukraine, one of the comments that summed up the new perspective of the youth group was, "These kids have so little, and they are happy. We have so much, and we are not." That was the beginning of acknowledging their need for more of God.

Work with the new church staff kept us busy. There would be planning meetings about the upcoming planning meetings. This new, fast-paced lifestyle didn't feel right, like David felt in Saul's armor. But if this was it, then we would do our best to adapt and make God proud. Our previous church was so different: there, it was like a grass fire that had the potential of going too far. Calgary was very professional, like church is business. Lance was away a lot, and I felt a little lost but was totally loving being a mom.

Most nights, I would wake up to feed our baby and rock her long after she had fallen back to sleep; I was completely overwhelmed with how much I could love another human being. I considered how it was like discovering a whole new ocean of love, and I whispered to my Lord, "I love her so much." Feeling my heart was no longer my own, I had lost every power to guard it.

He immediately responded to me: "Cindy, I love you much more than that." I was undone. I was reminded of the Scripture:

> If you, imperfect as you are, know how to loving-
> ly take care of your children and give them what's
> best, how much more ready is your heavenly Father
> to give wonderful gifts to those who ask him?
>
> Matthew 7:11 (TPT)

My heart-exploding love was evil compared to God's righteous heart. This was too magnificent to fully comprehend.

We were settling into our new normal when I knew I needed to establish an exercise habit. We were trying out a detox fad to lose the baby weight we had both gained. Awake at five a.m. so I could be back from the gym before Lance left for work, I was reading over the package instructions for how to mix a detoxing slime beverage when I noticed a warning on the label in bold: **DO NOT USE IF PREGNANT.** I kinda chuckled at reading that. I mean, that would be completely impossible. It took ten years to get pregnant, and I had a five-month-old baby sound asleep in the other room. The thought was ridiculous, but then I remembered that I had about one hundred extra pregnancy tests left over, so I thought, "No harm, no foul." I didn't want to be distracted at the gym, from which I was now officially procrastinating. I grabbed a stick and took the test just to ease my mind. *Tic. Tic. Tic.*

I waited for the one line to appear so I could get out the door, but like seeing police lights in the rearview mirror, there were two lines staring at me! I was puzzled and a little scared. I quickly did three more tests at the same time; it must be that the one I just used was faulty. Were my eyes deceiving me? Every test had the same result. I had only seen one positive test before this, and that was to confirm the life of our beautiful, strong-willed tornado! A downpour of outrageous extravagance crashed over me. A memory of when I was nine years old surfaced. My mother knew how much I wanted an Easter dress, and I had my eye on a long dress with cap sleeves and lace trim in the Sears catalog. She surprised me by buying two, one in each color, red and blue. There, in that bathroom, at 5:30 a.m., was when I genuinely understood God is never miserly or withholding. He does not settle for being a fair God. He is a lavishing, extravagant, above what you can ask or think, good Father. As a bonus, my Lord also gave me the gift of being like a normal wife who gets to share the secret with her husband.

I woke Lance, who, by the way, is not a morning person. He couldn't wrap his brain around what I was saying. (This would have been fixable if he drank coffee, but that's another story.) "How did this happen?" he asked, completely bewildered.

I held the pregnancy tests in my hand and said, "The old-fashioned way, baby!" I bet that's what happened to Zachariah, John the Baptist's father. I bet he just couldn't wrap his head around how it was possible that, after all those years, his wife would be pregnant. How? And why now?

On my very first Mother's Day, the day I had hated for the past eleven years, I was now a mother as well as pregnant with another child! I'll be honest; I did not see that one coming. When I read about Elizabeth and Mary conceiving near the same time, under completely different circumstances, but relishing the same joy and wondering how a God so big could see women so small, it resonated. Elizabeth said, "'How kind the Lord is!' she exclaimed. 'He has taken away my disgrace of having no children'" (Luke 1:25, NLT).

Always, expectations are partly better than anticipated and include results that we did not anticipate at all. I went to a mom and tots group to get out of the house and have some social connection. My little girl, who loved to sing, blow bubbles, and give kisses at home, was not the life of the party at the moms' group. I carried Kenzie into the community center and found a cozy room with stations set up for the children: blocks, dolls, coloring, toys. There were beanbag chairs scattered about so moms could visit while being at the toddler's level. It looked perfect. I don't know if it was only-child syndrome or if she was so advanced she had arrived at the terrible twos early, but she terrorized the little group, not just the other toddlers, as she stomped around grabbing toys, pulling hair, and baring her teeth like an angry chimpanzee. Even the mothers would back off when she came close. I had imagined sipping coffee and throwing my head back with laughter with my new friends; this was nothing like that. I lost sight of her for one minute but then located her in the fireplace, sitting in years of ashes, swinging her arms, creating her own little dust storm, and singing, "Do you know the muffin man, muffin man..." I was so frustrated I wanted to drop her off at Drury Lane! That was a delight to clean up. In the very next unsupervised moment, she found her way to the men's restroom and was discovering the urinal. Surprise, no one asked to exchange phone numbers with me.

When I arrived home, I was met by my overconfident husband who sang-talked his question, "Sooo... how was your time?"

"I'll tell you how it was; it was terrible. No one would talk to me. They were afraid for their children's lives. She was one continual threat, hitting and grabbing. And they looked at me with judging eyes that said, 'What kind of mother are you?' And the truth is, Lance, I agree with them. I can't handle her, and now we're having number two! What was God thinking?"

Just then, Kenzie, completely oblivious to my exasperation, toddled into the kitchen, dragging her blanket, and said, "Mommy says, "Grr!" Daddy says, 'I ove ou!'"

Lance scooped her up and tried to laugh it off.

Truthfully, I was worried. Expectations get me in

trouble a lot. I expected my daughter to be shy and quiet. I thought I would teach her how to blend in. But this girl was not like me; she wanted to stand out. What was I in for?

How baby number two changes things. The first baby's weight, height, and every progression was documented in the baby book. Each achievement celebrated weekly. With the second pregnancy, the ultrasound appointment snuck up on us; time was flying. We were excited to see what was happening inside and know the gender.

The ultrasound technician pointed and told us to, "Look right there between *his* legs."

We didn't scream or cry. We looked at each other and shared the same thought, *"Crazy prophet lady was right!"* Well, if I live to be one hundred, I will never understand how God does this. Eternity may be enough time to figure it out.

We were told by a few people that we had a million-dollar family. Why, thank you very much. That sounded like a grand compliment. We didn't realize the saying came from the fact that if you have one of each, you're going to need a million dollars to raise them.

Again, my age made the delivery a high risk, and our son was breech, so we had a C-section date set. It was nice to know the date instead of wondering, or in my case, obsessing.

Our gentle, kind-hearted son was just fourteen months younger than his sister. From the moment he showed up, Lucas, with his dark cocoa eyes, has been a complete heart-melter. Because of the C-section, I had two nights in the hospital alone with him. I should have used the time to rest, but I marveled at what a wonder he was. I woke up to see him, lying awake, looking around so peaceful and unassuming. Within twenty-four hours, I could see he had the opposite personality of his sister. I pulled him close and whispered, "Lord, what is it about him?"

I sensed a warm, pleasing smile of response. "He will pray big prayers and see big answers." I had learned not to attach my interpretation to the words of God, so I wrote them down so one day I could look back and see how that would look.

Lucas is the seventh-generation grandson of the Canadian Fathers of Confederation, which greatly pleased his grandpa.

I nicknamed Calgary the city of no sleep. The baby

stages were a blur. How was I? Busy, emotional, and tired all the time. Was I happy? Absolutely happy, but oh, so tired.

The most common encouragement people would try to give me was the ever-popular, "Enjoy it. It goes so fast!"

I would agree, nod, and smile, but inwardly reply, "This week did not go fast, and I don't see next week going fast." Hindsight is always 20/20, and now I agree that it went fast, too fast. I remember looking at my babies and trying to imagine what they would be like, how they would look, and how their personalities would develop. Now, I look at them and just marvel at what they have become.

Two babies so close together left me lots of work in the physical goals department, so I began to try again. Only one person finished behind me in my first 10K race. For years, I had dreamed of being a runner, the intense kind whose feet glided along with the smooth cadence of an Arabian stallion. I had always loved running, but I was more of a 5K girl. A 10K race was over the top for my novice skills, but I was not running for the winner's medal. I was running for my two-year-old daughter, Kenzie. The fertility clinic had organized a charity run.

After my ten-year journey of waiting to conceive, hoping, praying, and pushing past adversity, I felt the 10k was a symbol of what happens when you just don't quit. The quote, "Pain is temporary, but quitting lasts forever," was my mantra during the run. Running longer than you have physical stamina feels like drowning. It takes all you have to resist surrendering to the swells. To me, infertility had felt like the scarlet letter "I," the cloak of shame that was immovable. With every kilometer, God was reminding me of my journey: the hope, rejection, weeping, anger, confusion, words of encouragement. Through it all, he was faithful. I wish I had behaved better during the waiting, but I would never trade the experience of growing in trust and love with my Lord. As I neared the finish line, my friend Melody was there with my two babies cheering me on. I crossed, completely out of breath and bawling. Life was perfect.

Everything in my being resists change; to say I love routine is to say that I love breathing. I had a nest that felt cozy and safe, and now I was ready for the happily ever after. How I loved the security of feeling settled! I could see the proverbial sunset, "And they had two near-perfect children, lived in a grand city, and grew into a boring senior couple who were still madly in love. The end."

8.

∽

HOUSE OF HONOR

If any of you lacks wisdom, let him ask God, who gives

generously to all without reproach, and it will be given him.

But let him ask in faith, with no doubting, for the one who

doubts is like a wave of the sea that is driven and tossed by

the wind.

James 1:5–6 (ESV)

The wind blew in off the mountains so suddenly, sending chills through my bones, and the hollow whistle had an eerie feel like coyotes howling in the distance. The wind was sent to displace my nest. The dream job we moved for in the first place came up short; the senior pastor resigned. Lance is fiercely loyal, and he was committed to do his best to keep things running well. At the same time, my dad, who was pastoring in a northern community, was considering retiring. He called Lance and invited him to transition to the role of senior pastor. Lance was not interested in a lead pastor position; he felt he would be a youth pastor until he died. I was relieved that he said no. I know my husband; he is a city boy. I also know northern communities, and I did not see this oil and water mixing.

Lance received a call to preach at a youth camp less than an hour from Cold Lake, the community where my parents lived. My dad invited Lance to preach at his church on the Sunday following the youth camp. We were happy to see my parents and for our babies to have grandparent time.

The night before we drove into Cold Lake, Lance had a dream. We were in the forest, and he saw a rider on a white horse. In the dream, he said, "Cindy, look."

I replied, "Lance, look up," and he saw the same image of a white horse and rider in the sky.

He woke up and asked the Lord, "What do you want to tell me about that dream?"

He felt the Lord saying, "On earth as it is in heaven."

It was still a puzzle. He knew the dream was from God. We agreed to keep it in prayer until we knew the meaning.

The words *familiar* and *family* are from the same origin, meaning from the same household, and that is how we felt when we walked into the Cold Lake Community Church; we both felt like we were home. You could never have convinced Lance to shift from youth to senior pastoring and to move to a small community, but the spirit of God led him into the next season of his destiny. The church in Edmonton had been emotionally heavy. The church in Calgary had been program heavy. God was leading us to a place where his spirit would balance naturally. Both previous churches had prepared Lance to lead spirit-filled with a strong foundation.

Our home in Calgary, the gift from God, had more than doubled in value. We looked for a home in Cold Lake, and there was not much available. It actually came down to two choices: one with a hot tub in the basement (insert image of moldy, rotting walls) and a beautiful family home with a big yard, a fully-developed basement, and a two-car garage. It was a dream home. I was resisting, as usual. I felt it was too big. I also knew someone was going to have to clean that beauty...every single day! We realized that this was our only choice, and to our delight, our offer was accepted, and the transaction was almost an even swap from our previous home to this one.

It did not take long for Lance to see that there was a giant learning curve, but within months, the church was growing rapidly. God gave Lance the direction he was seeking. Instead of retiring, my dad stayed on and trained Lance while planning to switch roles; Lance would become senior pastor, and my dad would be the assistant. My parents had a small home not far from us, and with the housing shortage, it was a perfect time for them to sell. Lance presented the idea that they move in with us, and we make the lower level of our home a suite for them. This was all happening fast. I was worried about being too close.

I loved my parents; I didn't want this to go sour. Lance and I were far from perfect. What if we had a massive blow up? I knew there were benefits to having my parents close, but there were dangers too. In the two minutes I had before Lance picked up the phone to invite my parents into the rest of our lives, I prayed an I-hope-this-is-you-God prayer, and so sweetly I felt the words, "Honor your father and mother, so that you may live long in the land the Lord your God is giving you" (Exodus 20:12).

My parents were tickled to be so close to the kids and became our greatest asset in ministry and in raising our family. Their living with us made it possible for me to be involved with the women's prayer ministry. My mother was like my fairy godmother with the house cleaning. I know God provided the perfect home for us to meet all our needs.

As for Lance adjusting to a small community, my worries disappeared the day he told me he was going to shoot gophers with a bunch of guys from church! Who was this man? When he got home, I asked how it went, wondering if I would have to pull out the boxes and start packing again. He said, "Cindy, I looked at the truck and the guys with loaded guns ready to drive through a farmer's field, and I knew if I joined them, there was no going back. So I jumped in and had the time of my life!" The city boy became a great hunter. I knew God was still in the miracle business, and I could burn the moving boxes.

One thing we had not considered when we moved from utopia city to smallville was how perfect it would be to raise a family in a rural area. Things like walking through the forest became one of our favorite family things to do. Now, every fall, the crunchy leaves remind me of the early years and those walks with those beautiful chubby faces. Those were rich times together.

And so I began to do what I am amazing at: I settled in, organized my world, and I was happy. One day, I opened the mail, which always arrived by noon (I am that fanatical about routine!), and I was surprised to find a letter from the fertility clinic marked confidential. It was a bill to continue the storage of the unused embryos. Wow, I had totally forgotten about that. I guess because we felt complete, and with the second pregnancy from natural conception, we didn't think of ever needing the clinic again. But here we were, staring at this piece of paper, wondering which box to check.

Option one: continue to store the embryos for the low price of $99.99. Option two: donate the embryos to science—no way. Option three: request they be destroyed—double no way. Option four: the thaw option—thaw to donate to a couple or thaw to use ourselves. We, knowing full well the anguish of barrenness, had looked into the logistics of donating to another couple, but because of one of the procedures during the initial extraction of the eggs, the embryos did not qualify as donation quality. In fact, that procedure made the embryos possibly not viable quality for our use as well. We were basically told that they would do an embryo transfer for us only, but it would be a waste of money and not recommended. They gave a strong warning not to be hopeful. That clinic will never be accused of giving false hope on my account, so we proceeded to waste their time and our money, but how could we choose anything else?

Here we go again. Upon thawing, the twelve embryos became three that were viable to implant. That may sound like plenty, but it was actually a very low number. It was comparable to scoring the one winning lottery ticket out of ten million.

We were low key about the whole thing. We already had a great life, but there was a giddy excitement about, "What if." We almost felt it would be too much to hope for. We knew, for us, destroying the embryos was not an option, so we felt this was the only answer. We made an appointment to go back to the fertility clinic.

The seven-hour drive gave me time to think. I looked over at Mr. In-the-Zone and smiled. I had been thinking about this very quandary of how one could go from raging inferno to quiet coals. Coals are good; no, they're great, but how long had it been since he looked at me and had a sense of wonder? I felt like I had waited so long for this but was this what I was waiting for? Our family life was great, and our ministry life was fulfilling, but what about us? Maybe I'm so selfish that it will never be enough for me. Can I not be happy with ice-cream; why am I the kind of girl who looks around wondering if there are cherries to put on top? I thought back to our first love, how it brought out the best in me. Inhibitions had fallen away, and I became the best version of myself. I think I actually became more attractive.

My being a very picky eater disappeared, and I found myself eating dim sum and laughing like a French clothing designer who overuses the word, "Dahling!" Who wouldn't? This fine specimen of a man had lingered on every word I spoke. His only want had been to conquer my heart. Twelve years, two kids, and many hunting seasons later, somewhere between "I can't live without you" and "Sorry, were you talking to me?", I again hated ethnic food, and I somehow became way less interesting.

There ahead was the big red sign; we were at our

halfway mark and bathroom stop. I ran in, and as I was standing in line to pay for my sparkling water (Yes, it was the longest line), I noticed a young man in panic. I could tell his payment card was not being accepted, and he was trying to reach someone on the phone. He melted my heart because he was so young. Since having a son, I had the habit of looking at all men under the age of thirty as someone else's little boy. He was getting nowhere with reaching someone on the phone, and by this time, I surmised that he was driving a work vehicle and needed to be somewhere soon. I'm sure this was the long line I was supposed to be in that day. I stepped up, handed my card to the cashier, and discretely said, "I will get his bill," simultaneously sending a flare prayer to God: "Please let him not be driving a tanker truck." I quickly left, not wanting the awkwardness of him saying thank you; I hate awkward! The clerk was not good at keeping secrets, and the young man came charging out of the gas station just as I was closing the truck door. I saw him coming and just blurted to my husband, "Drive, Drive!"

"What's your problem?" He went immediately into classic fixer mode; fixers always want to identify the problem first.

"Just go!" I banged the dashboard, wondering if Bonnie and Clyde had communication issues? "Go!"

That's when the desperately grateful man knocked on my window and yelled through the tinted glass, "Please, can I talk to you?"

I shook my head and mouth the word no. One more time, I growled, "Quick, get moving! Go!"

The persistent young man now begged, "Please, I just want your phone number. I want to call you. Can I get your address?"

At that instant, my husband's eyes grew big as saucers. Now, he definitely found me interesting. I savored the moment before telling him I had paid the young man's bill. The understanding washed away his instinct to teach the shameless stalker some manners. My husband lowered the window and told the stranger, "Don't worry about it. Bless ya, man." As we drove away, he chuckled and said, "I thought…"

I cut him off, "Yeah, I know. That was funny."

He reached for my hand, and the quiet coals warmed me. "God, thank You for that," I inwardly prayed. "Twelve years was a long time to be married, but it was not too long."

The procedure was very quick because we didn't have to go through the growing eggs stage. It was like a dental checkup with no concerns: in and out. Then we waited. The egg was already fertilized, so we'd find out if the procedure was successful about fourteen days after implant day. If the test result came back negative, there was a chance it was just not showing up yet, and we'd try again in a couple of days. But if it's positive, well, we'd have the winning ticket, and we'd be one in ten million.

I thought I knew our family song, the rhythm of our family. This only proves how oblivious I was to how families constantly unfold and evolve. I was so wrong. God is always more than we can ask or think.

This was a different pregnancy; I was over forty and had gestational diabetes. I believe later-in-life pregnancies are more common now, but then I was a concern to everyone. We kept quiet about it until we passed over the first twelve weeks; we wanted to be sure. We had a couple over, friends from our church, who had three children. Lance was out back with the husband, and I was inside chatting with the wife. Without planning it, we both asked them what it was like having the third child.

Lance's conversation went like this: "So, do you recommend having a third child?"

"Man, it is chaos. Don't do it! With two, you each have one to be in charge of, but the third one just makes life crazy." He obviously thought we were in the deciding stage.

Lance replied, "Oh, well, Cindy's pregnant."

He gulped, "Ah, it's actually great; you will love it."

The difference between men and women could be seen by the contrasting conversation inside. I asked my friend, "So, what's it like having three children?"

She gushed, so happy to tell me of the joys: "The older two adore the baby. It's so great to have a little one; the baby stage just goes too fast. It's the best decision you could make."

"Wow, that's so good to hear because guess what? We're expecting again!"

She jumped up, hugged me with tear-filled eyes, and said, "Congratulations! That's so wonderful." It was a sweet feeling to have another gal rejoice with me.

One of my dearest friends, Jenny, was a nurse

and also in a high-risk pregnancy. We both had two other young children and would get together with the whole brood. In the chaos, we would find the company therapeutic. One of God's greatest kindnesses to me has been in unexpected friendships. Often, I assumed someone was just an acquaintance, but they would become a heart sister.

Liberty Brooke was born three years after her brother. She was a joy-filled, dark-haired, beautiful girl. Again, I am amazed at how three children can have the same parents and be so different from each other. I cannot imagine our family without her. On her birth day, while we were still in the delivery room and after she had been weighed and measured, the doctors left, and it was just us and one nurse. Lance held our cocooned baby girl as he walked her back and forth singing, "How great is our God." I wondered if we had chosen the right name and if it would be symbolic in her life.

The attending nurse said, "Oh, by the sound of that song, you must go to church."

Lance replied, a little tongue in cheek for my benefit, "Yeah, I try to get out every week."

Then the nurse went on to say how she used to

go to church, and she really missed it, but she hadn't gone for a long time. She even opened up about the reason why she quit going: a deep hurt from a leader in her church. In the next moment, Lance asked her if he could stand in the place of those leaders and ask her for forgiveness? She began to cry as Lance asked her to forgive those misguided people because Father God missed her far more than she missed going to church.

She nodded her head and said, "I do forgive them." Everyone was crying. She tried to regain her professional posture and commented, "I could get in big trouble for this."

Lance said, "God planned this meeting. Be blessed in his love for you."

I could see the transformation of peace on her face. I was in awe at how God showed us right in that room after Liberty's birth that, yes, it was the right name, and this is what it will look like, "freedom to those bound by lies and restoration of broken hearts." Liberty continues to grow in this gift of compassion today.

Home, healed, and happy, I was back in the saddle of ministry. I was preparing for a ladies' conference: speakers, worship team, and all the committees needed to be successful. I worked late in the evening creating lists and making sure everything was covered. The next morning, I woke up early with a Robin Mark song in my head. It was a new favorite song at our church about deliverance and following after Jesus.

I was running out of time to secure a speaker for our conference because I was leading ladies' morning Bible study, which made the issue even more real. Lance and a fellow minister, Dan, popped by the church.

The friend of Lance's from America said to me later that day, "Cindy, the ladies group seems to have something really special happening there."

Because it was my most prevailing thought, I spilled out, "Yeah, but I'm desperate to find a speaker for our upcoming conference."

In his male, problem-solving tone, he replied, "I know a lady who would be perfect: Rhonda Calhoun. You should call and ask her."

"How about you call and ask her?" For me, this was a big deal for me to suggest; I was desperate.

He called her right there, and to my absolute delight, her response to him was, "Dan, if they are friends of yours, I'll do it." I didn't know one thing about the woman, but I felt like she saved me.

That was the most powerful women's conference I have ever been a part of. There was such a presence of God's heart to set ladies free of wounds and the lies of the enemy. At the end of the conference, I was presented with a painting from one of the ladies from our church. It was a soft watercolor of me as a shepherdess, holding a lamb in a pasture scene. I knew God was calling me to a deeper place. He was transitioning me into partnering with him in caring for his beloved ones.

It's amazing how that in the midst of our busy lives, God is never busy. He is organized and right on schedule, tying up loose ends and bringing everything full circle. He works all things together for good. Fifteen years from the time of hearing God say, "Cindy, I am also the God of Sarah, Rebecca, and Rachel," I received a card of thanks from a lady who attended the conference. When I pulled the card from the envelope to find the exact same stationery card with the picture of the shepherdess from years before, it felt like a holy moment. I had tried to find that stationary for myself a few times over the years, but it was no longer in print. I guess God had one copy set aside for me on that day to remind me that his plans for me remained the same.

I was growing in our women's prayer ministry. A

few ladies, who, like me, had been healed of past hurts, helped in these healing prayer sessions. Rhonda, the speaker from our ladies conference, had taught us that our heavenly Father wanted to walk and talk with us every day as he did with Eve in the Garden of Eden. This was a spiritual revelation that held an anointing for freedom. I could say to a struggling lady, "God loves you," and it would be mildly received, but if that woman heard, "I love you," from God's heart directly to her own heart, it was life-changing. In my personal prayer time, I experienced a season of great growth. Instead of occasionally hearing his words, I heard them daily. I was in a newlywed season of insatiable hunger for more communion with my Lord.

One Sunday morning, I was in my closet, the only place to hide from my family. I was enjoying my Lord's tangible presence. I could see a picture of Jesus and me sitting on a park bench. We were just chatting and enjoying the sunshine. We were eating ice cream cones, and it felt so real. I was telling him how happy I was and that I didn't understand how this was so real. I asked him, "Am I making this up? Is this real?" I kept these prayer encounters to myself. I was worried they would be criticized, and in truth, I didn't want them to end. In the picture, I saw Jesus look at me and smile. As I was finishing my ice cream, I saw something at the bottom of the cone. It was a blue gumball! Jesus did it again. He more than answered my question. When I was a child, we had ice cream cones called screwballs. I had completely forgotten about them. The part that made them so enjoyable for a child was the surprise at the bottom. I knew he was as close as my breath, and this was more real than the floor I was sitting on. It was as if I could ask him any question, and he would tell me the answer, but there was no answer worth shifting the moment.

I looked at my watch and told Jesus, "Oh, no. I have to go. I'll be late for church!"

Jesus laughed at how I leaped from wonder to work and replied, "Really, Cindy?"

Then I laughed at the irony. There was an easiness to perceive God's presence that was childlike: no formula, no distractions, no guilt.

We had everything we dreamed of and more. The rhythm of our lives was found in Ephesians: "Now to the one who can do infinitely more than all we can ask or imagine according to the power that is working among us" (Ephesians 3:20, ISV). This lavish display of God's faithfulness presented us with a daunting sense of our inadequacy to raise these little ones and to fulfill their destinies.

God gave us a powerful key: we learned about the power of blessing. It was more than praying for your children; it was speaking life, destiny, and promise over their very spirits. Not just a one-time event; it had become a normal part of our home. Prayer is usually spoken toward God, and all eyes are closed, but a blessing is spoken to the person you want to bless, face-to-face, eye to eye. We would bless our kids at the dinner table weekly. We would bless whoever was at our table and if they happened to be there on their birthday, even better. My parents enjoyed participating and watching our children grow in this new family tradition. It became something everyone looked forward to, and by the age of three, our children could speak blessings over each other as well. We made a list of family values. We asked the question, "What does it mean to be a Steeves?" We came up with honesty, fun, and grace, but the top of the list was honor. It's been the key to raising our family by teaching them that we honor well. All we say and do stands under that umbrella. We honor God and others. We strive to make our home a safe place. The world is quick to tear them down, we want our home to be different. We aren't through yet, but we are working at it, and we are committed to a foundation of peace in our home.

We found a fantastic deal on a repositioning cruise, sailing from Vancouver to Los Angeles. We had always wanted to take our children to Disneyland and thought, "What a way to do it!" But even with the reduced fare, it was a lot of money for the five of us. A friend encouraged me by saying, "Cindy, when your kids grow up, they won't remember a new carpet or paint, but they will remember a family adventure!" Disney is known for being a step above everyone else in service, and we were not disappointed.

At that time, Liberty was four, and every crew member would address her as "Princess." After a few hours of every passing staff person saying, "Hello, Princess," she turned to her dad and asked the obvious question: "How do they know I'm a princess?"

We were all on the upper deck enjoying a family dance party with all the favorite Disney characters, and Lance leaned over and reminded me, "Remember, before kids, how we said if we ever do have a child, we'd want to do this?" Wow, he reminded me of the desire we had in our hearts. I also thought of the emptiness I used to carry, which now seemed a lifetime ago.

After ten years of serving in the northern community, our church had become our extended family. The grass was greener nowhere else. I had everything. There was nothing to wait for, just a life to be enjoyed. But my nemesis always shows up when I am comfortable. My man, who had the world by the tail, became unsettled. At first, I thought a vacation would fix it, but the unsettledness grew to question whether he was even supposed to be a pastor anymore. Lance had always been the strong one. Maybe this was burnout. He began struggling with insomnia. As much as he willed himself to dig in, he could not get out of this low. I knew the heaviest weight on Lance was how a life change would affect our family, and I also knew I had the key to unlock that weight. If I would tell him, "It's okay if you leave pastoring. If the decision is a mistake, it's okay if we fail. That's part of life." Those words could free him. I just needed to believe they were true first.

I had to find my peace with God in this. Did I trust God with my life or not? Did I trust him with a new life as much as I had come to trust him with this life? I went to my prayer room to release all my worries.

Jesus showed me a picture of him and me looking over a cliff. I felt a weight of an alarm clock in my hand. The bells on the top were heavy. I could feel the knobs to wind it on the back; the hands on the face were controlled by the knob in the center.

As I lifted it to inspect its purpose, Jesus spoke: "Cindy, who would you like to be in charge of your future?"

That was easy. "Of course, I want you!"

He smiled his all-knowing smile. "Okay, go ahead and throw the clock off the cliff."

I looked at the clock and then the cliff. What was wrong? I want God to be in charge. I've learned to trust him; why was this so hard? Why was the clock still in my hand? I looked back at Jesus and saw what he already knew. I trusted him when life was calm and I knew the routine. But in truth, I want what I want. I need to be in control. How could I be so oblivious to my gaping, flawed heart? I felt like I just found that my dress was tucked into my pantyhose. Did everyone else know this about me? I was ready to run away and hide, ashamed of my false confidence.

Jesus spoke tender truth: "Now that you know

what's held you back, you can choose to be rid of it if you want." Jesus didn't bring me here to shame me. He knew overcoming required confronting.

I looked at the clock. It appeared to be smaller, rusted, and defective. I lifted it with ease, and strength beyond my ability enabled me to throw it so far, and it seemed to shatter into dust. A free heart is better than all the security the world has to offer. I could tell Lance that I was ready for whatever was next.

Lance had a friend in town who did team-building and coaching. Sam had been in ministry his whole life, so it didn't take him long to pick up on the weight Lance was carrying. Lance confessed that he felt it was time to quit pastoring.

Sam asked, "Have you thought of going to a different church?"

"Absolutely not! This church and community have everything. If I can't be happy here, why go some place else?"

Sam knew this was not a discussion to win, so he simply said, "Why don't you pray, 'God, if you're speaking, I'm listening.'"

Lance asked if I would pray with him. I, the "good

wife," agreed. It was a sweet little prayer; what could happen? In the ten years we lived in Cold Lake, Lance never had other churches ask him to consider another pastorate. The week after that simple prayer and Sam leaving, Lance received three, *three*, calls of inquiry.

The first call was from a city in Montana! Nope, too far. The next one was from a church in Saskatchewan, the province right beside us. This had to be it. God would want me close to my parents; after all, he's the one who taught us about honor. The last call was also from America. Also, nope. I asked Lance if we could take a drive to Saskatchewan to check out the new community. His response continued to confirm that opposites attract, and God never gives me the easy plan.

Lance said, "Honey, I just feel we need to follow through on the first call, and if it doesn't work out, we move to the second."

It's as if he knew that speaking to me calmly only infuriates me. "Crazy talk! What about my parents? What about that thing called a border? What about Americans who run around with guns on their hips? The mafia? Our three innocent children? Lance, what if by the time you figure it out, Saskatchewan is gone?"

"Then we trust God." His eyes were so vulnerable as he spoke, I knew I lost, and I knew he was right.

My morning routine of being still and listening was interrupted by an out-of-place thought. In the same background music I had listened to for so long—the quiet, soaking music—I heard the faintest line jump out at me: "Leave your father's house." Hmm... I wonder if that's in the Bible. I don't recall it. Not that I'm that familiar with every line; it is a big book. I checked it out, and the passage from Psalms says, "Now listen, daughter, don't miss a word: forget your country, put your home behind you. Be *here*—the king is wild for you. Since he's your lord, adore him. Wedding gifts pour in from Tyre; rich guests shower you with presents" (Psalm 45:10, MSG). That was what I needed; the words pierced my heart, and I knew my Lord was saying, "Yes, this is from me." I can fly further on one phrase from God than a thousand kind words from people. At once, I told Lance, "Sink or swim; I'm all in. If this works out for the better, great! If not, we have another chapter in our story, and we still have us."

The chats, then interviews, with the church in Montana was making moving a very real possibility. We had a weekend off and decided to go spy out the land. Neither of us had ever been to Montana, so it was a sixteen-hour road trip adventure. We crossed over the border in darkness, and after an hour of swerving roads, the sun began to rise. Cue the singing angels. It was glorious! The rock walls were perfectly split through a canyon where a river roared down its winding path. The colors of the sunrise were exceptional: orange, gold, and pink. God displayed his finest artwork that morning.

Lance's sister, Nadine, called. I hoped it wasn't bad news; this was early for her to call. She was excited to tell me she had a dream that Lance and I had a baby boy. She said, "It was so real, I had to tell you." One of the issues that pulled at my heart was the thought that leaving Cold Lake felt like leaving a family behind. It was as if God was saying, "would you leave one child to spend time with another?"

I secretly hoped if the land was ugly and the people cold, maybe Lance would pull the plug, but so far, Montana was flowing with milk and honey, and the chances of the congregation being cranky in such beautiful places were slim. We had seen some of the prettiest and most rugged landscapes I have ever laid eyes on. Cattle grazing on the hillsides, many deer and antelope sightings. (Antelope are adorable.) Bozeman, our destination, was surrounded by mountain ranges in every direction! I had a crazy thought, *I'd love to see the view from the very top.*

We settled in our hotel and looked around town. There was a historic, bustling Main Street, a community theater, epic ice cream venues; everything was sadly perfect! We went to the Sunday service hoping to get a sense if this would be a good fit, a confirmation to continue the process. Only a couple of people knew who we were, so it was fun to just blend in and observe. We were warmly greeted with big smiles and bigger hugs. We found seats near the back; it sounded familiar and felt comfortable. At one point in the service, the congregation was encouraged to greet each other, and a beautiful lady with red hair noticed we were new. She greeted us with such genuine interest. She wanted us to know that the church was currently without a pastor but in the process of looking. It was hard not to reveal who we were. This conversation showed the character of this body because she cared enough to let us know of the current situation. We were impressed.

The weeks passed, and we received an invitation for Lance to speak, and a vote would follow the service.

We waited in an office while the vote took place and was then tallied. Someone had slipped us a card with a picture of Canada Geese on the front, and on the inside was written, "Honk, honk, honk." It seemed someone was already cheering us on! The vote was a 99 percent yes. We were thrilled. So many gifts were delivered to our hotel: flowers, fruit, chocolate, balloons, and bags of Montana gear from mostly anonymous friends. This motivated the front desk clerk to say, "Can I ask who you are?" She thought we were somehow famous.

I told her we would soon be pastoring a church in town.

She replied, "Wow, I have to check out that church. They sound fun."

We were told by the very expensive immigration lawyer this process will take three to five months, so we put the house on the market. Listing the house was like waiting for the Lord's return: you clean it up, wait, and every morning you think, "Maybe today," but you still have to live in that house, so every night you make sure it's ready again, just in case. We announced our resignation at our current church and were completely overwhelmed with the love and sentiments of our Cold Lake family. Goodbyes are difficult and healing. We will treasure our season there like gold in our hearts.

We packed the house and outfitted the local thrift store. Month five was upon us, and it came and went. This was so reminiscent of waiting for summer to come. A familiar knot grew in my chest: what if the visa doesn't come; what if we are refused? The house sold in August, and there was no word about our visas. We stayed at a friend's house, daily thinking, "Surely today." It is one thing to impose on family and friends, but to impose with a family of five and a large dog!

Lance did some speaking at a church where his friend pastored. The honoraria was a blessing to our family. One sermon was from Luke, chapter 7, about John the Baptist and how he was the one to proclaim the Messiah's coming. But when he was in prison, discouragement set in, and he sent word to Jesus asking, "Are you the Messiah we've been expecting, or should we keep looking for someone else?" (Luke 7:19, NLT) I could identify with that expectation. The point of the sermon was: if God's not rescuing, listen to the message. You can feel despair and choose to trust his word. The message Jesus sent John was apparently exactly what he needed to hear because John remained faithful until the end. Discouragement is a spirit that is evicted by truth and hope.

We stayed in five temporary locations and ended up in a cabin in the woods. (The dog was very pleased with that location.) We had over one hundred days of waking up everyday thinking, "Today, the visas will come." It was a roller-coaster pattern of being hopeful Monday to Thursday and then not-so-hopeful Friday to Sunday. (Word about visas never came on weekends.)

One day I just blurted out, "God, I don't think there is anything else left in me to ring out. What do you want from me?"

His answer came as refreshing as the scent of the surrounding pines: "Why do you believe your life has been on hold? There is just one variable you have been obsessed with: location. Have I not provided every-thing you need? I have hidden you away for a season to enjoy your family and to rest. If you were *there*, what would be different? All the things you value are right in front of you. You know what you want, but can you trust me to provide what you need? This is not a delay to me."

I saw a picture of me sitting in a classroom. Jesus was the teacher, and I saw two drawings on the chalk-board. One was an amazing fruit and vegetable stand with fresh, choice produce like at a farmer's market. The other picture was like a Sunday school flannelgraph of an Old Testament altar of large stones.

Then he spoke the heart-revealing question: "Cindy, why was Abel's sacrifice acceptable?

I had done hard time in Sunday school; I knew the answer, "Abel's sacrifice was what you required."

"You, like Cain, think you can decide what obedience looks like in your life. And, like Cain, if you will bring the right offering, will I not accept you as well?"

My heart released like molten lava. "But Lord, what you require of me is broken and messy. I can't make myself behave well. I can't make myself trust you!"

He patiently led me through the process. "I don't judge the outward; I look in your heart, to lay your ugly brokenness before me costs you. It's the risk of being laid bare, the risk of knowing you are not enough. The honesty of who you really are is incense; it is a sweet fragrance that rises to my throne. It captures my heart. I will set my fire on that sacrifice, and out of those ashes, the purest gold will surface."

"Lord, I know you are right. I'm just so sick of

circling the same struggle again and again. I feel so broken in my ability to surrender."

Like a proclamation trumpet, he filled my heart with, "One day, you will know the joy of surrender—my spirit in you and not of yourself.

So, I settled into homeschooling, as horrible as I was at it, and every day we went for walks in the woods outside the cabin. The children loved checking on the progress the beavers had made during the night. We had s'mores for lunch from the wood stove and family dance nights. Lance and I stayed up late and enjoyed the majestic star-covered skies that could never be seen from a city. We learned the names of the fifty states. (Who would think you could have such laughter teaching an eight-year-old to say, I-oh-wa!) This pleasure could have been lost if I had not practiced the simplicity of living in the moment. Being present is so much better than waiting.

I once learned that in some Asian cultures, silence in conversation is a sign of respect, that you are savoring what was spoken. Our culture has lost the value of waiting, and any invention that saves time is an instant success. Yet for all our "saving," still no one owns tomorrow. To remind myself that waiting is a gift, I tried to let people go ahead of me in line at the coffee shop or in a checkout line, and I take a look around because I don't want to miss anything. Discipline in the way I dream of it may never be mine, but a life theme of waiting has brought joy, and since I've embraced it, I feel stronger. One tiny grain of sand is an irritant, but if you wait long enough, it will become a pearl of great price.

The weather was getting colder, and the cabin was not built for winter. We knew the owner would have no choice but to close it up soon. It was a Saturday, and we knew there was no word about visas on weekends, so we headed into the city for distraction and Starbucks. Lucas said, "I bet we'll hear today."

Not wanting to squash his faith, I said, "It's got to be soon, son." We were standing in line at the coffee shop; I was ready to drown my cares in a venti. Lance stepped out of line and walked outside to take a call. (Honestly, that man! Has he never heard of voicemail?) I so desperately needed coffee. Our kids always did this: they'd ask me why daddy did something when they knew I had no more information than they did. I told them the obvious: "He got a call. He'll be back."

When Lance returned, the first thing I noticed was

his flushed cheeks. I knew it! It must be the visas, but it was Saturday, so what was this about? "That call was from Montana. The visas are in." The relief washed over us all.

I wanted the details because I'm a woman, "How are we hearing today?"

Like the punch line to an obvious joke, he said, "In Montana, they get mail on Saturdays!" (Canada does not.)

The smile on Lucas's face was brilliant as he chimed in, "That's pretty cool, hey, dad?"

9.

◦◦

HERITAGE HOUSE

"The lines have fallen to me in pleasant places; Indeed, my heritage is beautiful to me"

(Psalm 16:6, NASB)

Within a few days, we were living in a valley surrounded by mountains. That giddy feeling returned, and it was not just due to an adjustment to the altitude. Our kids were overjoyed with a longer summer break. We noticed everyone had an accent, although they couldn't hear it. We obviously enjoyed celebrating July 4th, Thanksgiving with the wonder of green bean casserole, and, of course, mail delivery on Saturdays. Lance was the only one who could be employed because of our visa restrictions, and the Lord provided a parsonage in which we could live. The church was planning to sell the parsonage right next door, so it had been recently renovated, and we were blessed to have a comfortable and convenient place to stay. Our family began hiking, and the excitement of conquering new trails and, eventually, mountaintops was exhilarating. I was living a dream from so long ago, so far removed from me. It was indeed a miracle. I picked up a rock from every hike and put the name of the trail and the date on it. I have found a few heart-shaped rocks, which only encourages my crazy love and confirms that God must be okay with my obsession.

After living in the parsonage for a couple of years, I had gotten stronger and moved on to more challenging hikes at higher altitudes. I had seen photos on social media and heard from friends of the Beartooth Wilderness. Locally, we could hike for four to eight hours and be rewarded with a view of a lake or waterfall. But on the Beaten Path in the Beartooth was an abundance of waterfalls, rivers, pristine lakes, and rugged terrain with a climb of over ten thousand feet in elevation. A trek that far would require twenty to thirty pounds of gear and take a minimum of three days with zero cell service. Well, I knew I was nowhere near that experienced, and mostly I thought, *"Wow, God, wouldn't that be something?"* I have come to realize God counts many of my thoughts as prayer requests, and he begins working on them right away.

This past summer, a friend told me that she and her husband were doing the Beartooth hike; it would be a three-day adventure, and I was invited to join them. It is one thing to imagine yourself taking a selfie on top of a mountain and completely another to have your bluff called when you don't even own a tent or sleeping bag. There were no bathrooms and no cell service, but there was one plentiful thing out there: bears! I told her I would think about it but ended the call already knowing my answer. I heard an old cynical voice with a very familiar question, "Who do you think you are?" I felt I had no business going out there. I was not experienced, a wimp when it comes to discomfort, and the lack of a bathroom for three days was enough to seal my no. I was sad. If only I were ten years younger.

It was getting closer to the trip date. If only Lance could go, too, I would feel comfortable. That way, I'd have someone I love by my side as I drew my dying breath if this was to be my ticket out. But Lance was involved in a summer production at the community theater and was a definite no. I did consider the courtesy of mentioning this to God in prayer, then at least

I could give my final answer as, "I prayed, and it's a firm no."

So, I prayed, "God, I have this silly idea. I want to do something I've never done before that looks nothing like me. I know I'm not made for this. If only my husband could go, I would do it in a heartbeat."

I felt him say, "Why don't you ask a friend?"

I went on to whine about me not being camping material: "I'm over fifty. Is this when I start sleeping on the ground? And three days with no bathroom, I mean, I know people handle it all the time, but sometimes I have to go at three in the morning."

He clearly spoke: "Cindy, you don't have a bathroom problem. You have a fear problem. Are you going to let fear steal the gift I have for you?"

Hearing him so clearly gave me courage. I knew if he was encouraging me to go, I would be okay. I knew he would be with me, and he was giving me permission to go for it.

I asked my friend Tamilla, the one who joined me on most of my adventures. Although I knew she had to work, I thought I'd try. I was surprised she did not say no immediately. She said she would see if she could get the dates off. She did not own a proper backpack or tent either.

So, within a few days, Tamilla and I were in the local camping store booking rental gear and looking at dehydrated food! The thought occurred to me that perhaps we should have a practice run at setting up the tent, and our sales associate obliged. He gave us the exact tent we would be renting and confidently told us the set-up time was five minutes, tops. Twenty minutes later, he finally rescued us and showed us the tricks that make things so easy—when you know them! He also politely declined our offer to pay him to come along, carry our packs, and be on constant rescue alert.

Day one arrived, and we all met at my home bright and early. I was spoiled with a lovely breakfast made by my husband. I did have the thought, I hope this isn't my Last Supper (breakfast). We weighed in with our backpacks and found we each had a whopping twenty-eight pounds to carry over the next three days! I had lost and gained that a few times over my life, so I could now see that I had been in training for this day. Lance and I had dropped a vehicle off at Red Lodge, the ending point trailhead; Ana and her husband, Rich, would drive us in their car to Cooke City, the starting point trailhead.

We drove two hours to the trailhead and made use of all the rest stops we could along the way. (I was secretly hoping I could pre-eliminate as much as possible.) We parked and put our packs on. Water, camera, and bear spray were all handy, and we were feeling strong.

Tamilla said to me, "You know, this actually feels pretty good."

I agreed, "Yeah, me too!"

Rich, our fearless, much-experienced leader, said, "Yes, but you're still in the parking lot!"

We headed onward, bursting with adrenaline. I admit, for all my concerns, the first hour felt so normal. We came upon hikers who had started the trek from the other side and were near their end. I asked, "How was it?"

A man with a thick southern accent said, "All I can say is I hope you have strong bug spray. If not, go back and buy some. The flies and mosquitoes are horrible." He mentioned he was from Louisiana. (Don't they have swamps there?) If he thinks the bugs are bad, what am I doing? I did at that moment regret bringing only a small bottle of Off because I was concerned that my pack was too heavy.

Rich seemed to be looking behind us a lot. After another mile, he confessed that the map didn't completely download on his phone, and we may have possibly taken a wrong turn. The only way to be sure was to go back and confirm. We added another couple of miles to our hike to find that, yes, we were on the right path. This was not discouraging. I was so happy to be there, to be doing this, not just reading about it on someone else's social media page. I felt so alive. We reached our first camp to set up for the night. As Tamilla and I were setting up the tent, it began to rain. We were pleased that we remembered the steps, and it looked like a real tent.

The food of choice for this trip was dehydrated, so we just had to boil water and wait fifteen minutes for the magic. I was fascinated with the concept but not so much with the taste. The best dehydrated product was the ice cream bars; you just eat them straight out of the package. They were crunchy, but the flavor was exactly like an ice cream sandwich. If I'm ever in this situation again, I will fill my pack with them.

The next morning, we were up early. Hearing a little mouse scurrying around my tent zipper during the night may have contributed to my low REM sleep, but no cell service meant I couldn't check my sleep app to be sure. We ate dehydrated eggs. (I may have found the secret to weight loss! I won't be writing the company to tell them they're doing fine work in the survival world.) We packed up like pros and hit the trail. The weather changed every half hour from fog to rain, to outbreaks of the sun. I wanted the full experience of what backpacking was really like, and I was getting it. The higher we climbed, the more spectacular were the views. At the top, the temperature dropped, and we were surrounded by peaks. We passed lakes that looked like they were untouched. The trail was diverse: at times, we crossed grassy fields, and as we gained altitude, there were places the path was so narrow and rocky I thought my mother would not be happy if she knew where I was.

Every step, I realized that this was really happening: I was doing something I thought was impossible for me. I was breathing freedom. Waterfalls were plentiful, and every turn had a new wonder to display. We all had our favorites: Ana loved the waterfalls, Tamilla was taken with the wildflowers, Rich liked the rivers and probably would have liked us, girls, to walk a little faster and take fewer pictures. I loved it all, but seeing the ginormous rocks took my breath away. I would scream and say, "Wow, you guys, can you believe how big this one is?" I could not imagine grandeur more than what I had already seen. There just couldn't be anything better.

I was at the front of our single-file line, and my head was down as we passed through thick trees. I was holding branches, so they didn't snap back. As I cleared the trees, the trail immediately became an open expanse, and I found myself in what looked like a natural rock amphitheater. As high and as wide as I could see was rock, huge slats like tiers of seats, and high cliffs like walls. The rocks had stripes that provided a beautiful contrast to the deep gray. I stood in the most holy place I have ever been and whispered, "Oh, my heart. This place..."

Instantly, my thoughts were acknowledged when I heard my Lord say, "Cindy, I've waited forever to show you this."

I was flooded with the understanding that the one who gave me the crazy love of rocks had watched over me my whole life, and he knew me in my mother's womb. He knew when he created this very place that this moment would be one of the best of my life, and I will treasure it forever. To think I could have missed it because of fear. A Scripture came alive to me: "Fear will never conquer me for you already have!" (Psalm 23:4, TPT). I realized that during my whole life, I'd felt like I had to wait, but I never considered that my Lord was waiting for me.

"Now I know that I am for my beloved and all his desires are fulfilled in me" (Song of Songs 7:10, TPT).

Epilogue

Have you ever considered the theme of your life? I wanted my theme to be joy, strength, or, dare I hope, discipline. But my experience has been that life themes are given, not chosen. As I look back over the years of barrenness, my greatest regret was that I didn't enjoy the goodness of God in the waiting. I wasted so much time in self-pity. What I've learned is that no one owns tomorrow, not the richest person, not the healthiest, not even the most fertile. Hannah was barren in body, and God healed her, but Peninnah was barren in spirit, and that was far worse. We only have today, and the one who holds tomorrow says, "Today, my grace is sufficient."

I recently read an article by J. Dianne Datsun from sciencing.com. Dianne says house sparrows are named that because they like to live near humans. They are opportunistic eaters, and humans provide many opportunities. A female sparrow weighs less than one ounce and eats approximately a quarter of its body weight each day. Have you seen a sparrow eat a crumb of bread? That little crumb is life to that bird, but what is that crumb compared to a whole slice of bread? What is one slice compared to a loaf? Compared to a corporate bakery?

I began hearing God's voice in my heart as a child. As I grew, so did the clarity of his voice. As I matured, he often spoke to me through Scripture, songs, and sunsets. Then there was the season he met me in my imagination with vivid pictures. Now, journaling conversations has become a daily communion with my wisest and most faithful friend.

A lifetime of growing in trust brought me to a place of comfort, maybe I took this comfort for granted and started thinking I deserve a good life. My heart was revealed to me recently when I experienced a bike accident, and I broke my arm and wrist in four places. My response to that horrific crash was, "Why did this happen?" In reality, it was, "God, why did you let this happen to me? I thought we were close?"

I was lamenting to my dear friend Mona because she's always on my side when I'm in the depths of self-pity. Mona is classy and conversely cute as a button, her 80 plus years and blonde coiffure often flow with wisdom and wit. She surprised me with her response: "Cindy, why do you think God didn't warn Joseph about Potiphar's wife?"

Wow, of all the examples she could draw from! I had ten possible answers rolling in my head. Perhaps a few were correct, but in my heart, I knew the answer had to do with Joseph going to the lowest place so he could be trusted in the highest place. God didn't abandon Joseph; he developed Joseph. God's ways are always higher than ours.

Now, I imagine all the wheat fields in the whole world for all of time. In each exchange with my Lord, I am the house sparrow whom he feeds from his endless supply. To me, it's life, it's everything. He loves and cares for the sparrow, although he knows the sparrow will never comprehend the vastness of who he is.

This in no way says that my encounters with the Lord are insignificant. Rather, it speaks of the tremendous love of the Creator, who is enthralled with this sparrow. My Lord is all-wise and all-faithful. He is a true friend, and He is Yahweh, the name regarded by the Jewish people as too sacred to be spoken.

A new level of trust was the beginning of developing new depth in me, but I found that there is no true arrival. It's a lifelong journey of increasing my trust as well as my capacity to be trusted. I'm no longer baffled by, "Why did God let this happen to me?" Instead, I choose to be extremely grateful that my accident happened when I was enjoying life and living because every day—every crumb is a gift.

To those who hurt so deeply because your arms are empty, who have lost babies, or are not able to conceive again, I remind you not to fall for the lies of your enemy, that you are being punished, you are not good enough, or the lie that God is unkind. There is nothing that can separate you from God's love. Don't give up. Don't do what I did for so long and run from God. Run to Him. His arms are wide open, and they are full of comfort, healing, and strength. His love for you is so vast, it cannot be measured. Your Lord is committed to you knowing and trusting Him, even if it takes a lifetime.

CPSIA information can be obtained
at www.ICGtesting.com
Printed in the USA
JSHW041722310521
15340JS00002B/3